GEORGIA HEARD

The Revision Toolbox
TEACHING TECHNIQUES THAT WORK

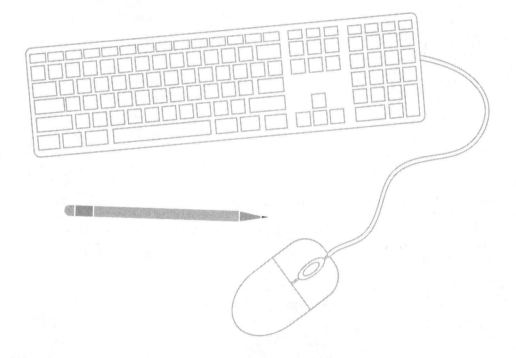

Second Edition

HEINEMANN
Portsmouth, NH

Heinemann
361 Hanover Street
Portsmouth, NH 03801–3912
www.heinemann.com

Offices and agents throughout the world

The author and publisher wish to thank those who have generously given permission to reprint borrowed material:

Excerpts from the Common Core State Standards © Copyright 2010. National Governors Association Center for Best Practices and Council of Chief State School Officers. All rights reserved.

"Dragonfly" from *Creatures of Earth, Sea, and Sky* by Georgia Heard. Copyright © 1997 by Georgia Heard. Published by Wordsong, an imprint of Boyds Mills Press. Reprinted by permission.

Library of Congress Cataloging-in-Publication Data
Heard, Georgia.
   The revision toolbox : teaching techniques that work / Georgia Heard. – Second edition.
      pages   cm
   Includes bibliographical references and index.
   ISBN 978-0-325-05689-0
   1. English language—Composition and exercises—Study and teaching (Elementary).
2. Editing—Study and teaching (Elementary). 3. Language arts (Elementary).   I. Title.
LB1576.H327 2014
372.62'3—dc23   2013044134

Editor: Zoë Ryder White
Production: Vicki Kasabian
Cover and interior designs: Monica Ann Crigler
Typesetter: Kim Arney
Manufacturing: Steve Bernier

Printed in the United States of America on acid-free paper
18 17 16 15 14 PAH 1 2 3 4 5

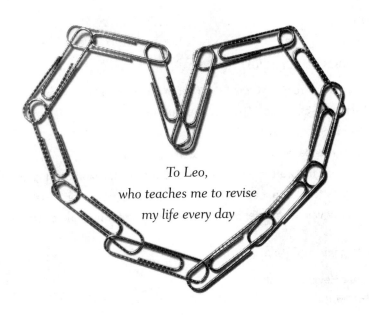

To Leo,
who teaches me to revise
my life every day

Contents

Acknowledgments

When I think of every person who guided me, directly or indirectly, in writing this book, I imagine a large family tree. Not a small linden tree but a great oak like my uncle's family tree, which he painstakingly researched and which is now (unrolled) almost as long as a football field. Like me, this book has many ancestors.

Since the "roots" of this book are extensive, and it would be impractical for these pages to be as long as a football field, I'll name only the most recent "branches" of the tree—those people who directly guided me in writing this book. I hope that those of you not specifically named will know how grateful I am to you for all you've taught me about writing and teaching writing throughout the years.

I want to begin with a special thank-you to the editors of the first edition of *The Revision Toolbox: Teaching Techniques That Work*, Bill Varner and then Lois Bridges, without whom this book would never have been written eleven years ago. I also want to thank my wonderful and wise editor of the new edition, Zoë White, without whom this new edition would never have been written or finished. Her discerning writerly eye has made all the difference in helping me think more deeply about revision. I also want to thank Team Heinemann for supporting my writing and giving me the opportunity once again to send my words out into the world—especially Patty Adams; Vicki Boyd; Eric Chalek; Monica Ann Crigler; Michelle Flynn; Lisa Fowler; Vicki Kasabian; Anthony Marvullo; Lesa Scott; and Beth Tripp.

I'm grateful to the Benjamin School teachers and administration for their continuing support of my work; to the teachers around the country and around the world who took my online revision course a few years ago through HeinemannU and offered invaluable feedback, suggestions, and student examples; and to the many hundreds of schools where I've had the privilege of witnessing students who were engaged in the soul work of revision.

This book would not have been possible without the love and support of my husband, Dermot. And finally, thanks to my son, Leo, for the joy and daily revisions you bring to our life.

Introduction

I wrote the first edition of *The Revision Toolbox: Teaching Techniques That Work* in 2002 when my son was three. It was difficult to imagine then that he would be a teenager someday—fourteen years old, six feet one inch tall, towering over me with his low voice. It was also difficult to imagine moving from my home in Manhattan to Florida. I've learned a lot in these past eleven years—every minute a treasure. One thing I've learned for sure is that life, like writing, is all about revision. Revision of our expectations, of our dreams, of the blueprints we make in our minds of exactly how our lives' paths will go.

As I've continued to both write and teach writing over these past eleven years, I've made revisions to my thinking and to my practice of teaching writing, but I've also come to realize that many of the ideas and suggestions in the original edition of *The Revision Toolbox* still hold true; the essentials of writing stay the same.

In this new edition, I've kept some of the same stories that appeared in the original edition because my learning and thoughts about revision derive from those experiences, but I've also layered in anecdotes and ideas from the present time.

One of the things that still holds true is the trepidation (maybe *dread* is a better word) that students feel about revising their writing.

I know the feeling well. When I first learned to write, the teacher assigned a topic, and as we wrote, she paced the classroom and periodically stopped behind my desk to read what I had written. I waited nervously, hoping for a few encouraging words.

More often than not she said what I feared: "It's not finished yet. I think you should add more." I was devastated. I often harbored hopes of having just written a great short story or essay, and my heart sank upon hearing her words. For me, this meant one thing: my piece of writing wasn't good enough. I sat there not knowing how or what to add or change. It was at those moments when I thought to myself, "I guess I'm not a real writer because real writers don't have to change their writing."

"I think you should add more details" is a familiar line that many of us remember hearing from our teachers. For many young writers, these words do indeed imply "Your writing is not good enough." A student's writing may very well need some work, but the real problem is that our students don't know how to revise (even if they want to) because they don't know any specific revision strategies.

The most frequent questions that I still hear from teachers are, "How can I get my students to revise?" and "My students refuse to change anything after they're finished. How can I help my students know what to change?" I believe that as teachers we have good intentions. We know what our students' writing might need—details, character development, or more description—but most students haven't been taught the repertoire of revision strategies that they need to make the changes.

We must welcome young writers into the world of revision through invitations and tools that make revision concrete and tangible. We must remind students that the writing process *is* revision. Revision isn't merely the act of making a few cosmetic changes. Revision is a way of seeing and then reseeing our words, training our eyes and ears to recognize what good writing sounds like, and learning and practicing strategies that will make a difference in our writing.

Education has changed radically in eleven years. (Who knows what it will look like in another eleven years?) Perhaps the biggest change is the adoption of the Common Core State Standards by most states, which has moved writing to the forefront. One of the biggest shifts in teaching writing is the move away from a focus on personal narrative and toward nonfiction instead.

In this new edition, I've added specific revision ideas and strategies that pertain to the three genres emphasized in the CCSS—opinion and persuasive writing, informative/explanatory writing, and narrative writing—not only because they are identified in the CCSS but because many writing teachers seek out revision strategies for nonfiction as well as narrative, and these three genres are important and worthy for students to learn to write.

The CCSS include revision standards under "Production and Distribution of Writing" as follows:

CSS.ELA-Literacy.W.3.5, 4.5: With guidance and support from peers and adults, develop and strengthen writing as needed by planning, *revising*, and editing.

CSS.ELA-Literacy.W.5.5, 6.5: With guidance and support from peers and adults, develop and strengthen writing as needed by planning, *revising*, editing, *rewriting*, or *trying a new approach*.

CSS.ELA-Literacy.W.7.5, 8.5: With some guidance and support from peers and adults, develop and strengthen writing as needed by planning, *revising*, editing, *rewriting*, or *trying a new approach*, focusing on how well purpose and audience have been addressed. (NGA Center for Best Practices and CCSSO 2010; emphasis mine)

Although revision is mentioned in the CCSS, no specific revision strategies are identified. To "develop and strengthen writing" by "trying a new approach" or "rewriting" is exactly what writing is all about. Writing and revision are really one process: this is what we do as writers.

The point of learning about revision is not necessarily to make changes to every piece of writing, nor to write dozens of drafts. Students need to be able to bring the tools of revision to their writing the way a carpenter comes equipped for a job with a toolbox full of tools. Ultimately, the point of learning about revision is to learn how to help our writing convey more accurately what's in our hearts.

CHAPTER 1

Transforming Our "Revision Vision"

The topic of revision has elicited a multitude of not-so-enthusiastic responses from my students over the years.

"But I like what I wrote the first time."

"You mean I have to change my writing?"

"I like it just the way it is!"

Many students have stereotypes of what revision is or isn't. Most students see revision as punitive. Some young writers see revision as what they have to do when the teacher thinks their writing isn't finished. And many beginner writers believe that revising and editing are the same thing.

Revision involves making substantive changes to the meaning, content, structure, or style of a piece of writing rather than the more surface changes that editing demands. Revision means to have a vision of what we want our writing to be like. Real revision is inner work: clarifying what we really think and believe about an idea; getting at the heart of a story; distilling our sentences and words to best express how we feel and what we think. Revision is how writers write.

Every writer has her own process of revising. Some writers rehearse and revise in their minds before they write a word. Some writers write a quick first draft and then go back and revise. Others carefully compose word-by-word, revising in their heads as they write. Some writers write multiple drafts, while others write just one or two. Many writers view revision as playful and creative, and others dread it.

Revision strategies can also vary depending on the genre. Some nonfiction writing might be vague and unspecific; therefore, revision will consist of adding more specific language, facts, and descriptions. In narrative writing, perhaps the writing hasn't gotten at the heart of the story, so revision will consist of rewriting the narrative or characters with more clarity. Essay writers might revise by adding new ideas to support their thinking.

Students also need to understand that revision won't necessarily take place *after* they've finished a piece of writing; instead, revision will most likely occur *throughout* the writing process.

Currently, many writing teachers teach revision techniques occasionally or at the end of a genre study when students are finishing up their drafts. The two most popular, and sometimes only, revision strategies that we teach are adding details and cutting out unnecessary words. Just as we teach the craft elements of fiction, poetry, and nonfiction in genre studies, we need to model and discuss, and bring to the forefront, the processes and strategies of revision. We need to make revision a central part of the conversation and teaching in the writing workshop.

Given students' strong reactions about the process of revision, one of my graduate students suggested the need for teachers and students to amend our "revision vision."

The first step in transforming our revision vision is to be clear about our goals. I have four in mind when I teach revision:

1. To transform students' concept of revision from punishment to a natural and integral part of the writing process
2. To transform students' concept of revision from editing skills, practiced at the end of writing, to a process that occurs throughout all the writing stages
3. To transform students' concept of revision from an intellectual exercise (changing a word or two) to a more thoughtful process of rereading and rewriting to clarify what they believe, feel, and think

4. To equip students with specific user-friendly revision strategies, through conferences and minilessons, that each of them can independently apply to a specific piece of writing

Keeping these revision goals in mind, we also need to be aware of some of the essential ingredients that contribute to a successful writing workshop and how best to include the process of revision within the workshop framework.

Bring Revision and Process to the Forefront of the Writing Workshop

When I was in school, the writing focus was on making a perfectly spelled finished product and on publishing. None of my writing teachers in elementary or secondary school discussed revision. The attention was always on editing. Although it's important to complete a piece of writing, and it's deeply satisfying to publish, we need to switch the focus away from the final product to the process of writing, which, of course, includes the revision process.

How many times have we heard students ask, "How long does it have to be?" This question shows me that the students' priority is completing the assignment, usually with the bare page minimum rather than the number of pages it would take to fully express what they need to say.

When I get together with my writer friends for coffee, we spend time reading each other's work and talking about our revision processes rather than reading our finished pieces to each other. We might talk about another way we should begin a piece; point out which words are abstract or cliché; highlight a part that gives the reader a vivid image; or discuss what changes we need to make to improve our writing.

In classrooms, we can help ensure that process and revision become the central parts of the writing workshop if we do the following:

▸ conduct weekly "revision shares," where students share their work and ask for feedback about their processes and revision of their writing, or selected parts of their writing, rather than entire finished pieces;

Suggestions for Revision Shares

A student can try these techniques with a partner, with the whole class, or in one-on-one teacher–student conferences.

- Write and share three different leads and ask for feedback on each one. (See "Revision Lesson: Writing Compelling Leads" on page 58.)
- Share two different versions, drafts, or parts of a piece of writing, and ask for readers' opinions of each part or draft.
- Write part of the piece in different points of view and ask for opinions on each one. (See "Choosing the Right Point of View" on page 107.)
- Model aloud planning a piece of writing prior to actually writing.
- Share your process of writing and revising.

You might ask students to discuss a few of these questions in small groups or with peer partners:

What kind of reviser are you? Are you reluctant or eager?

Do you write a quick first draft and then return to revise? Do you compose and revise as you go along?

Are your revisions usually successful? Do they usually improve or clarify your writing?

What's the most helpful way for a reader to help you revise your writing?

How do you know when, where, and how to revise?

How many times do you usually reread your writing?

How do you know what to revise?

- encourage students to reflect on, and write about, their writing and revision processes in their writers' notebooks or on their drafts and share those thoughts with the class;
- share examples, quotes, and reflections from professional writers about their writing and revision processes (see, for example, Appendix A, page 117); and
- ask students to compose their own quotes and reflections about their writing and revision processes and share these with the class.

Invite Students to Share Their Thoughts About Revision

Exploring students' own experiences and sometimes negative feelings about revision will help open up the possibilities for revision. You might want to initiate a discussion by asking students to write about their feelings and experiences of revision and/or by giving them a revision survey (see Appendix B, page 119) as motivation.

Here are some highlights of several students' thoughts about revision, which they shared with me during discussions on revision:

being told it isn't good enough so do it over

that I have made really stupid mistakes

that I can't write it neatly enough (too many smudges)

that I misspelled the same word again

that I should have known better

Most students equate revision with failure rather than opportunity. And most students confuse revision and editing.

After a genre study on poetry, fifth-grade students responded to a short revision survey (see Figures 1–1 and 1–2).

As I've worked with students over the years, I've found that no matter what genre students are writing in, they often express negative feelings about revision and aren't aware of the many revision strategies available to them.

You might want to begin your introduction of revision by having students share their answers from a revision survey and then read aloud quotes by professional writers about revision so the students can discuss the differences and similarities between their thoughts and those of professional writers.

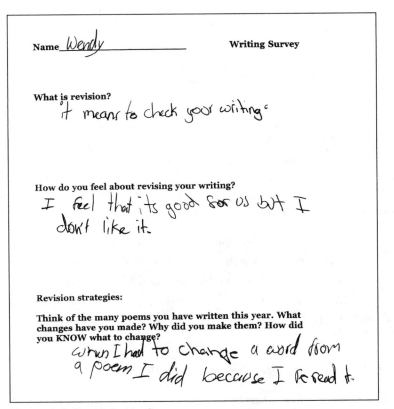

Name Wendy   Writing Survey

What is revision?

it means to check your writing.

How do you feel about revising your writing?

I feel that its good for us but I don't like it

Revision strategies:

Think of the many poems you have written this year. What changes have you made? Why did you make them? How did you KNOW what to change?

when I had to change a word from a poem I did because I reread t.

Figure 1–1 Wendy's Revision Survey

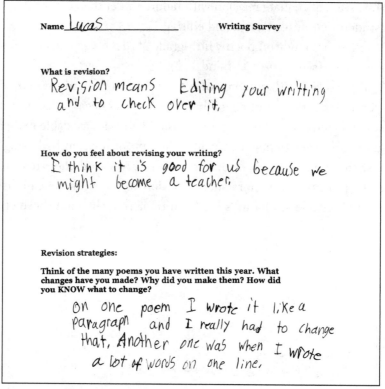

Figure 1–2 Lucas' Revision Survey

For example, when they hear this quote by Roald Dahl, students are always surprised at the number of revisions that Dahl made.

> By the time I am nearing the end of a story, the first part will have been reread and altered and corrected at least one hundred and fifty times. I am suspicious of both facility and speed. Good writing is essentially rewriting. I am positive of this. (quoted in Temple 2013)

And Hemingway's quote about "getting the words right" is a classic:

Interviewer: How much rewriting do you do?

Hemingway: It depends. I rewrote the ending of *Farewell to Arms*, the last page of it, thirty-nine times before I was satisfied.

Interviewer: Was there some technical problem there? What was it
                that had stumped you?

Hemingway: Getting the words right. (Hemingway 1958)

Teach the Purpose of Revision

Why do writers revise? Most writers revise because they realize that what
they have written doesn't match what they really intended to say. But not
every piece of writing needs revising, nor do writers want to revise a piece of
writing just for revision's sake. Writers revise because they feel committed
to making a piece of writing the best they can because it means something
to them—it matters enough to try to make it their best.

But how do you guide students in making sure that writing matters
to them? One way is by making sure that students can choose what to
write about.

Have Students Revise Writing They're Passionate About

It's much more difficult to revise a piece of writing that has been written as
an assignment, or copied from an encyclopedia, than it is to revise a piece
of writing that has personal meaning for the writer. If our hearts are committed to writing about a topic we're passionate about, revision comes easier. If we offer our students writing invitations that will inspire them, and give students choice in the topics they write about, students will become more person-
ally involved in their writing and, therefore, be more mo-
tivated and engaged during the revision process.

I realize that realistically we can't give students topic

Practice Revising with Existing Writing

A few months into the school year, you might ask
each student to select a piece of writing that he
wrote at the very beginning of the school year that
he would like (and feels a need) to try to revise using the craft and revision tools he has learned so far.
The writer can spend a day or two trying different
revision strategies to make the piece better.

choice 100 percent of the time. There are occasions when students must write on an assigned topic, but asking students to choose their own writing topics is a powerful motivator that will give them the confidence they need to become more fluent and independent writers.

Teach Minilessons on Craft and Demonstrate Specific Revision Strategies

Revision teaching and craft teaching go hand in hand. Craft is the art, skill, and knowledge writers bring to writing. In fact, many craft lessons are really lessons in revision. Having a continuing discussion of what makes up the qualities of good writing and demonstrating these qualities in minilessons will help students appreciate good writing.

If we expect our students to revise, we must provide them with specific strategies with which to revise. We can teach and demonstrate specific revision strategies by modeling our own and professional writers' writing and revision processes and by teaching minilessons that include revision strategies.

Expose Students to a Variety of Good Literature Through Mentor Texts

Every writer must gradually develop an ear for what good writing sounds like. By encouraging the reading of quality texts during independent reading time, reading aloud good writing, and modeling excellent literature in minilessons, teachers can help students foster an appreciation for good writing, which will guide their own revision processes.

Mentor texts are used by a writing community to study craft, genre, and other aspects of writing, and they can give young writers a vision of the kind of quality writing that is possible.

Students can also learn to read texts like a writer. Ask students to find places in a text that move them and to identify specific craft effects that the author uses. My book *Finding the Heart of Nonfiction: Teaching 7 Essential*

Craft Tools with Mentor Texts (2013) delves into this practice in more detail and has numerous examples of mentor texts that illustrate specific craft tools.

Help Students Develop Confidence, Independence, and Stamina as Writers

Students need to develop confidence, independence, and stamina as writers so they can begin to take charge of their own revision processes. In classrooms, we can encourage students' independence by

▸ giving students time to write daily;

▸ encouraging students to keep writers' notebooks, where they can record personal experiences, reflections, observations, questions, and so on and gradually develop a daily habit of writing;

▸ providing positive and constructive writing conferences and interactions with the teacher and fellow writers that will help pave the way for students' self-evaluation; and

▸ demonstrating the process and craft of writing in minilessons.

Revision can't be taught in isolation. Teaching revision depends upon all the many components discussed in this chapter to make it successful and integral to the writing workshop. (See Figure 1–3.)

Once students understand that most writing is rewriting, their concept of revision will change. Although revision requires deep reading and thinking, revision is when the real work and the real pleasure of writing begin.

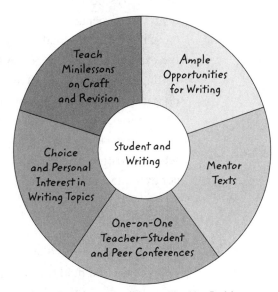

Figure 1–3 Components of Teaching Revision

CHAPTER 2

Revision Nuts and Bolts

Writing Center Revision Tools

My desk is stocked with all the tools I need for writing and revising. Most of my revisions occur as I write on my computer (cutting and pasting, deleting, etc.), but I still have real tools on my desk handy and ready to help me revise. For example, I have correction fluid for deleting words, scissors and tape for cutting and pasting, pens and highlighters in a variety of colors for marking up hard copies, three-hole paper in my printer for printing out drafts for a longer project, and a three-ring binder in which to place my manuscript.

Prior to conducting your minilessons and focusing on revision, you can set up a writing center with tools that will help support students' revision. For example, you might include these items:

- ▸ Post-it notes to flag passages, write reminder notes on, or write short elaborations on
- ▸ colored pens to highlight words, phrases, and sentences
- ▸ correction fluid to delete unnecessary words, phrases, and sentences
- ▸ flaps of paper and "spider legs" (long strips of paper) to cover up parts, to elaborate on, or to write sentences on and then tape to an existing text
- ▸ transparent tape to add sentences, tape flaps, and spider legs to an existing draft or to splice two parts together

- scissors to cut writing apart or cut out parts
- a thesaurus and a dictionary to help students find alternative words and look up unknown words (Many students might want their own thesauri and dictionaries at their desks.)

In your minilessons, you will be showing students how these tools can support their revision efforts. Ask students to suggest any other revision tools they may need.

You'll need to decide how and when students will use the revision tools in the writing center. Some teachers set up a separate revision center exclusively for students who are actively revising their writing to sit at and actually use the tools while there, and others provide the revision tools for students to take back to their desks. You might think about letting every student have a thesaurus with him at his desk while he writes.

Writing Fast Drafts

Oftentimes I suggest to students, especially when they're stuck, that they try fast drafting. A fast draft is a draft that's written quickly in one sitting.

Here are some of the reasons and situations in which students might try fast drafting:

- When students feel stuck, fast drafts help get ideas down on paper so they have something to work with.
- After students have webbed, or thought about their structures, fast drafts can help flesh out ideas.
- After students have researched and reread notes, they can fast draft to see if it reveals a possible structure.

Following are some of the guidelines for fast drafting:

- Decide beforehand how much writing you'll do in your fast draft: A whole page? Two pages?
- Before you fast draft, think through how your draft might go.
- Keep your hand moving and don't stop to reread or revise. Use what you know about writing in that particular genre as you fast draft.

Revision Partnerships

Writers need other writers with whom to talk and confer. Especially for revision, it's helpful to get another set of ears and eyes and to get feedback from your peers. To this end, you can set up revision partnerships with your students.

Each student can partner with one person, and then from time to time you can combine two pairs into a partnership of four. You might want to pair two students together who might seem different from each other but who can help each other as writers, or students can choose their own writing partners.

You may want to begin by asking partners to meet and work on drafts together after you give a minilesson on a particular revision strategy. Or, after students have worked on revision independently, they can meet with partners to share their work.

Partners can also work as sounding boards, modeling asking questions and giving positive constructive feedback that will spark revision. If you ask students to give constructive criticism on writers' drafts, you must model this technique first so it doesn't become a time for students to criticize each other's writing.

The Common Core State Standards state that students should use "support from peers" to revise their writing.

When students confer with peers, they might keep the following guidelines in mind (included in Appendix C on page 120).

Peer Conferring Revision Questions

Ask the writer:

1. What was it like for you to write this piece? Did you have any problems while writing?
2. What do you think you need to work on in your writing?
3. How can I help you? Are there any parts you want me to pay close attention to as I read or listen to your writing?
4. Are there any places where you can add more?
5. What is the focus or heart of your piece?
6. What will you work on next?

After reading or listening to a piece, tell the writer:

1. About a part that you think was well written
2. About a part that wasn't clear and confused you
3. What you think the heart or focus of the piece is
4. What suggestions you might have for adding or revising the piece

Revision Self-Assessment

After students have had some practice using specific revision strategies, they can assess their understanding (and we can assess our teaching) of revision by reflecting on and answering the following questions:

What have you learned about revision?

What revision strategy do you plan to work on in your next writing piece?

In the examples here, fourth-grade students show an awareness of the revision strategies that were most helpful to their writing and definite plans for strategies that they would like to try in the future (see Figures 2–1 through 2–4). Teachers can assess what revision minilessons have been the most effective to students' writing and understanding.

1. What have you learned about revision?
I have learned about Show Don't Tell, Strong verbs, and lots of slowing down time in Minute by Minute. All of them were very helpful the one I used alot was Strong verbs. Revison makes your story better and Magical. to
2. What revision strategy do you plan to work on in your next writing piece?
I think I want to focus more on cracking open words, and sentences. It will make my story more intersting and better.

Figure 2–1 Self-Assessment 1

1. What have you learned about revision?

I learned that when you revise, you have to give 110% for everything that you do. You can't be lazy or not care for anything, you have to open your eyes and add more magic to your story!

2. What revision strategy do you plan to work on in your next writing piece?

I would like to work on the minute-by-minute strategy because I love the idea of making your story worth while and slowing down time!

Figure 2–2 Self-Assessment 2

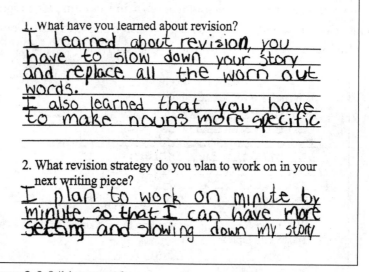

1. What have you learned about revision?

I learned about revision, you have to slow down your story and replace all the worn out words.
I also learned that you have to make nouns more specific

2. What revision strategy do you plan to work on in your next writing piece?

I plan to work on minute by minute so that I can have more setting and slowing down my story

Figure 2–3 Self-Assessment 3

1. What have you learned about revision?

    I learned about "show don't tell" and a lot
other. I think I learned a little bit more
about replaceing "Things" and I think I will
do that on my next piece. I also learned
about "Cutting out words" and finding new
words.

2. What revision strategy do you plan to work on in your
   next writing piece?

    On my next piece I think I will
work more on "show doin't tell" and "cutting
out new words." I think I will try
to indent a little bit more

Figure 2–4 Self-Assessment 4

Tips for Revising Electronically

If students are writing and revising on the computer, it's helpful to keep
these two tips in mind:

1. When students are revising, especially making large-scale revisions
    (reorganizing and changing a majority of their texts), they should
    be sure to save a copy of each of their drafts in case they don't like
    their revisions and want to go back to an earlier draft.
2. To help get perspective on writing, students might want to alternate
    between writing a draft on the computer and marking up a hard
    copy with a pen. Alternating modes, so to speak, can help writers
    see things they might not have caught the first time. (Be sure to
    have them print out the hard copies double-spaced so they'll be able
    to see and make changes more easily).

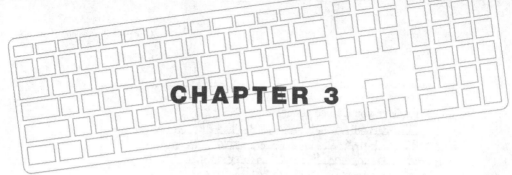

CHAPTER 3

Deep Reading

When we first moved to our apartment in Florida, I was amazed every day by the view out the windows—a 180-degree view of the Atlantic Ocean. I watched how the water changed from turquoise, to navy blue, to steel gray on a cloudy day. I slept every night with the windows open as I listened to the waves lull me to sleep. In my office, I moved my desk next to the window so I could see the ocean as I wrote. This was heaven! I made a vow to myself that I would never take this for granted; the film of familiarity would never dull my appreciation of the ocean's beauty.

Now six years later, I'm still in awe of the view, but that film of familiarity has crept in—even here. Sometimes my life gets so busy that I forget to see what's all around me. Often it takes going away and coming back to resee it. When I return from teaching or speaking at a conference (especially from the Northeast in winter), the first thing I do when I walk into my apartment late at night is open the balcony doors and breathe in the tropical sea air. I almost weep with joy as I stand and listen to the waves.

Sometimes we need to step away from our lives, and our writing, for a moment to be able to really see them. Maybe the point of traveling is to give us perspective on our lives so that we can see the people and things around us with fresh eyes. It reminds me of the Indian saying, "If you want to re-create the world, look at it with fresh eyes."

Getting perspective and really reseeing our writing are at the core of revision. Revision means "to see and see again." But to see again, we must learn to dig deeper and deeper into our experiences and thoughts. Some people refer to revision as "soul work" rather than simply an intellectual exercise of tightening verbs and deleting unnecessary words. Before we discuss any crafting revision strategies with our students, we must teach them that the first step in revision is to reread our writing in order to resee it. We are not reading to check for spelling or punctuation or to change a small word here or there, but to compare the accuracy of our words with what's in our hearts and minds. To be able to read your writing, then to stand back and measure it against your heart's experience or your mind's intention—that's the real point of revision.

As we discuss revision with our students, we must include strategies to help writers reread and resee their writing—to see their words objectively so they'll know what to revise. A writer must be able to look deeper and deeper into her writing, to peel away the outer layers to get to the core of what she's trying to say.

Reading our writing for the purposes of revision has some similarity to close reading of a text, where readers reread a text multiple times in order to come to terms with what it says and how it says it. A writer's purpose is different in that writers read their own texts to evaluate and analyze what they have written to clarify and strengthen ideas, experiences, and feelings.

When I write I usually begin by quickly getting words down so I have some text to work with. I might write a fast draft, a quick stream-of-consciousness draft, not worrying about how many pages or words I need or how long it will take me to finish. And then I tuck my writing away for a few hours, or a day, before I bring it out and reread it with new eyes.

Getting Perspective

One of the greatest obstacles of revision is that our words are often too close and we have no way of standing back and evaluating them because they're personal and they mean so much to us. The biggest question for me is, How can I reread my writing with a more objective viewpoint so that I can see the writing and not only the experience, content, or ideas

I'm writing about? That is, How can I get perspective on my writing so I'll know what to revise?

The following are two strategies meant to help writers gain perspective and objectivity on their writing, to make revision easier.

Listen to Your Words Read Out Loud

One way for a student to acquire a more objective view of writing and help assess what parts need revising is to listen to her writing read out loud. A teacher or another student could read it, or, if the writer is alone, she can record herself reading it and play it back. I usually ask the writer to listen to her writing without reading the accompanying words.

Students can also read their own writing out loud to themselves and listen for any places that don't make sense, or words that are vague or cliché, or parts that are well written, and take notes by highlighting these places with pens or highlighters. It takes practice for students to be able to assess their own writing, and they won't necessarily be experts at it at first. They might only be able to identify a word or two to change or an unnecessary phrase or sentence to cut out. It will be a gradual learning process as you model how to do this in minilessons and support their efforts in conferences.

Whether we listen to someone else read our writing out loud or read it out loud ourselves, we begin to hear the ebb and flow of our words and can assess our writing with more objectivity.

Refresh Your Eyes

Students can use the following revision strategy to help get perspective on their writing: Place a writing draft in a folder and let it sit until the next day (the draft could be a hard copy placed in a real folder or a draft written on the computer and placed in a virtual folder); then begin writing a new draft (without reading the previous draft). The next day, look at both drafts side by side and compare. Circle or underline parts of each draft that you think are the best parts of your writing and can include in yet a third draft.

When we write a second draft from scratch, it demands that we resee or retell our writing, and often new words, images, stories, and insights emerge in the subsequent drafts.

Large-Scale and Small-Scale Revision

There are two basic types of revision: large-scale revision and small-scale revision.

Large-scale revision is when a writer rereads a piece in its entirety and then reflects on larger, more general, revision questions, such as these:

Does this express what I really want to say?

Did I get to the heart of my narrative, essay, or text?

Does my piece have a focus?

Is my focus clear?

Does my organizational structure work?

Does my voice feel appropriate to the content?

This type of large revision usually results in rewriting a piece completely and can lead the writer to discover what he really wants to say. As the *Scott, Foresman Handbook for Writers* says, "THINK BIG, don't tinker" (Hairston, Ruszkiewicz, and Friend 2002, 61).

Small-scale revision is when a writer pinpoints a particular section or part of her writing that isn't working. For example, a conclusion doesn't work, or the writer needs to add more details in the third paragraph. This revision requires changing only part of the writing and then making sure that the revision fits in with the other parts of the text.

Getting into the Habit: Front-End Revising

Revision used to be taught as something writers did at the very end of the writing process. The writing process list I saw on many classroom walls looked like this:

1. Brainstorm
2. Write
3. Revise
4. Edit

The problem with this list is that it's not really an accurate description of most writers' processes. Most writers don't wait until their drafts are finished to revise because it's much harder to revise this way; revision becomes more laborious. If we break revision down into smaller pieces and revise as we go—sentence-by-sentence, paragraph-by-paragraph—it becomes more manageable. This kind of revision is called *front-end revision,* and we need to get students into the habit of revising as they write, not waiting until they finish writing their drafts to revise. So, what does this look like? It means getting into the habit of stopping after we write a bit, rereading, and reflecting on what we just wrote and asking ourselves, "Is this what I want to say? Is this how I want to say it?"

Writing and revising then become inseparable and are woven together as the same process. The writing process charts on a classroom wall might look like this instead:

1. Brainstorm
2. Write
3. Revise
4. Brainstorm
5. Write
6. Revise
7. Revise
8. Edit

Rereading with Different Lenses

When I was a teenager I used to love to try on sunglasses. I owned at least a half-dozen pairs, mostly because I thought sunglasses were cool and partly because each new pair changed my perspective of the world: the yellow lenses always made the world seem oppressive and murky like I was swimming under a dirty river; the blue lenses made everything seem cool and distant; and the rose-colored glasses made the world seem cheery and much warmer—especially in winter. I finally understood the expression "to look at the world with rose-colored glasses." In fact, sometimes I wore a pair of rose-colored "granny glasses" (these were small oval-shaped glasses that were popular when I was a teenager), and it always seemed to make me feel happy.

Stepping back and rereading writing is what authors do. I'll reread parts of my writing dozens of times—sometimes using different lenses each time, depending on the kind of writing I'm doing. Students can use this rereading self-assessment strategy for example after they've written their leads, after they have written several paragraphs, and also after they've completed their drafts.

After you introduce the lenses in a minilesson, ask students to return to their drafts and practice rereading their writing with a particular lens. Students can then share with writing partners any discoveries or revision possibilities they found through rereading. A few teachers have even created paper eyeglasses, each with a particular lens written on it, and placed them in a writing center for students to take back to their desks to help them focus on reading with certain lenses.

The Lens of Focus and Clarity

The questions, What do I really want to say? and What is the heart of my story or essay? are at the heart of revision.

Many beginning writers have a difficult time focusing their writing, and these questions can help.

Students can reread using the lens of focus and clarity by asking themselves questions such as the following.

Narrative

What is the heart of my story?

Is the heart or focus clear?

Are my characters developed?

Is my focus too big or too narrow?

Have I stayed on track for the entire piece?

Do all my details and anecdotes support my focus?

Are there any places where the language or details could be clearer?

Are there any places where I could cut out any words, phrases, or sentences that don't support my focus?

Persuasive or Opinion Essay

Is there a clear theme, thesis, or main idea to my piece?

What do I really think or believe about ____?

Is my point clear enough to the reader so he or she knows exactly what I believe and think about a topic?

Does every anecdote and detail contribute to my theme?

Are my supporting points clear?

Do paragraphs connect with each other to create a flow?

Informative or Expository Text

What is the focus of my topic?

What do I really want the reader to know about my topic?

What are the key pieces of information I want my readers to learn about my topic?

Which organizational structure will best support my focus?

Do I have supporting points, and are they clear?

Do I have text features that support my focus?

The Lens of a Stranger

Sometimes I try to pretend that I'm a stranger reading my writing. This pretend stranger could be an editor, or anyone I can imagine who doesn't necessarily know my story or my thoughts. As students read with this lens, they can ask themselves:

What would this reader think about my writing?

What would he or she want to change?

What part of the writing might be murky and unclear?

Does this reader understand what the heart of my story is?

Is my thesis clear?

The Lens of Language

Rereading with the lens of language means focusing on the words in a text—the meaning, sounds, and specificity of the words. Students can focus this lens even smaller and, for example, read with the lens of checking for active verbs or concrete nouns or read with an eye toward deleting unnecessary words.

Following are some specific questions writers can ask themselves, regardless of the genre they're writing in:

Is my language clear, precise, and concrete?

Are there any words that are abstract and vague?

Are there any words I can delete because they aren't necessary?

Are there any words that I overuse?

Are there words that I can "crack open" to expose other words that are more specific?

Are there any parts where I can elaborate and add more detail?

Are my verbs vivid and active?

Are my nouns concrete?

If I'm writing an informative or explanatory text, have I included any domain-specific vocabulary?

See Chapter 6 for more tips on using precise language.

More Rereading Lenses

There are many other lenses writers can use to read their writing for revision possibilities.

The Lens of Feeling

The lens of feeling helps you pay attention to the mood of the piece. Students might ask:

> Can the reader tell how I feel about my topic?
>
> Can the reader tell what my characters are feeling?

The Lens of Finding Your Best Writing

Writers can search through their pieces to locate the best parts and then strive to bring the rest of the writing up to that level. Students can start by rereading their writing and highlighting the best word, phrase, or line. Then, they can ask themselves:

> How can I get the other parts of the writing to be as admirable as this?
>
> Why does this part sound better than the other parts?

The Lens of Sound

When I reread for sound, I'm reading just for that—not for clarity, truth, or meaning. I'm focusing on the sounds of the words: what doesn't sound right; what sounds choppy; and what sounds wonderful. The question I ask myself is, "How can I make my piece sound better?" Tuning our ears to sound is something that takes a little practice. It's always easier to hear the sounds of our words if someone reads them back to us, or if we read them out loud to ourselves.

The Lens of *So What?*

The lens of *So what?* is similar to rereading for focus or clarity but goes a little deeper. As they're writing, and rereading their writing, students can ask the question, "So what?"

> Who will care about my story, essay, or research report?
>
> How can I get my readers to care as much as I do about my topic?
>
> If I add this detail, will it make a difference to my writing?

The Lens of Sentence Variation

Several sentences in a row of the same length can make writing monotonous. Students can reread their writing to see if they can combine any sentences to give their prose more life and rhythm and ask themselves these questions:

Are my sentences all the same length?

Do my sentences sound choppy?

Which sentences can I combine to make my words flow?

See "Sentence Variation and Fluency" in Chapter 6 (page 92) for more on crafting interesting sentences.

What Does Reading with Different Lenses Look Like?

Narrative

Here is an example of a narrative written by Emily, a fourth-grade student who had already made some revisions (see Figure 3–1). Since she is just beginning her story, let's try reading it with the lens of focus.

Bella, my little sister, Sophie, my eleven year old cousin, Granny, my grandma, and I finally got to my dad's house.

"I'm so glad you got to come over Sophie," I said as we jumped out of the car.

"Yeah, I'm glad I got to come," she answered. I knew she was happy to come over too because she had a big smile on her face.

We ran outside and I told them, "I have a bit of homework but it's easy so I can finish fast."

"OK," Bella sang.

I finished my homework and suggested that we play in the pool.

"That's fine with me," Sophie exclaimed.

We quickly got our bathing suits on and raced to the pool.

When we jumped in, Bella shouted, "It's cold."

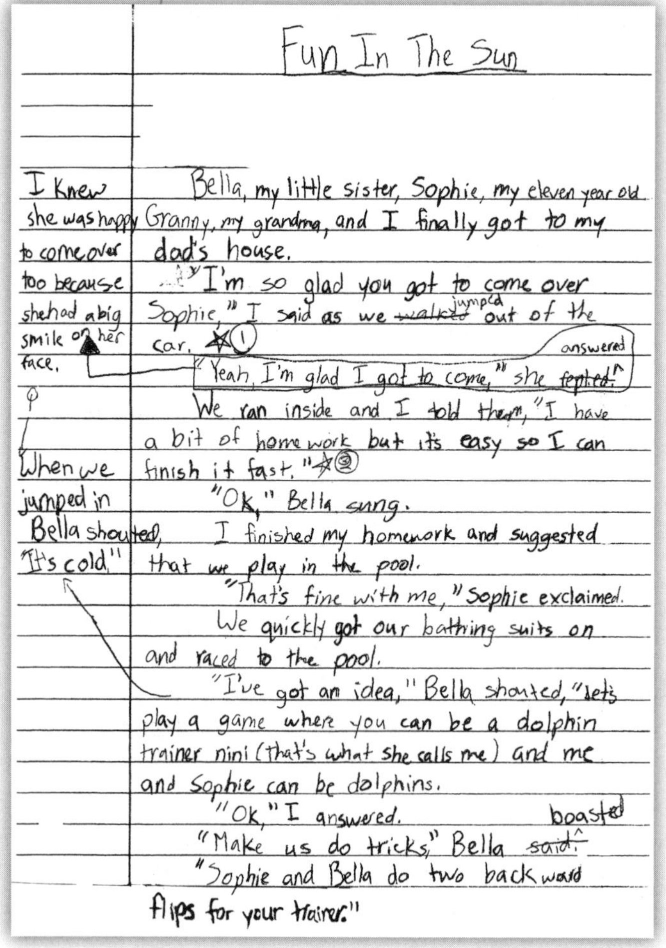

Figure 3–1 Emily's Draft of Narrative

"I've got an idea," Bella shouted, *"Let's play a game where you can be a dolphin trainer nini (that's what she calls me) and me and Sophie can be dolphins."*

"Ok," I answered.

"Make us do tricks," Bella boasted.

"Sophie and Bella do two backwards flips for your trainer."

It might be overwhelming for writers to ask all of the questions included under a specific lens, so Emily started with the initial questions from the focus lens as she reread her narrative:

▸ What is the heart of my story?
▸ Is the heart or focus clear?
▸ Is my focus too narrow?

After asking herself these questions, Emily decided that she wasn't exactly sure what the focus, or heart, of her piece was but told the teacher that it was probably "having fun." After a conference, Emily decided that having fun wasn't really the heart of her story; it was more like "having fun with [her] family." It was the connection to her family and the good times she remembered that were at the heart of her story.

If she had waited until her piece were finished before reading with the focus lens, she would have had to revise many of her details. Front-end revision is easier than back-end revision. By rereading her narrative early on in her composing process and asking herself what the focus of her story was, she was able to add details about other family members, including her granny and her father, to support the focus.

Information

This fifth-grade writer, Liana, wrote a quick biographical draft about a Native American artist named Carson Waterman. Liana was struggling with which lens would be most helpful in rereading her piece. The first lens she used was elaboration: Where are there places where I could elaborate? She reread and marked those places where she might be able to add more detail with asterisks, and her revisions are shown here in bold.

> Carson Waterman is a member of the Iroquois Nation. He lives in Salamanca, New York. In his paintings he has lots of designs.* **Carson paints people, animals, and Indian themes.** He uses lots of different colors.* He uses colors **like reds, blues and greens.** He is very strong in his artwork. I think his paintings really stand out. We watched a movie about Indian artists. In it we learned that there is a ninth clan.* **The Iroquois Nation divides themselves into clans that are represented by different animals.** The ninth clan is the eel. Carson Waterman is well known around the world.

After rereading with the language lens, particularly that of elaboration, Liana decided to reread with yet another lens: sentence variation. She felt her writing sounded too choppy when the teacher read it out loud to her. Here is her second revision:

> Carson Waterman is a member of the Iroquois Nation. He lives in Salamanca, New York. In his paintings he has lots of designs **such as** people, animals, and Indian themes. He uses lots of different colors **like** reds, blues and greens. He is very strong in his artwork **and** I think his paintings really stand out. We watched a movie about Indian artists. In it we learned that the Iroquois Nation **divides themselves into clans that are represented by different animals. The ninth clan is the eel which is Carson Waterman's clan.** Carson Waterman is well known around the world.

Letting Mentor Texts Guide Revision

As I drove home one day from running errands, and getting my car serviced, I heard F. Scott Fitzgerald's words fill the car from my newest audiobook, *The Great Gatsby*:

> In his blue gardens men and girls came and went like moths among the whisperings and the champagne and the stars.
>
> And so with the sunshine and the great bursts of leaves growing on the trees, just as things grow in fast movies, I had that familiar conviction that life was beginning again with the summer. (Fitzgerald 2007)

It was summertime, and I knew exactly what Fitzgerald meant by "life was beginning again with the summer." My son was away at camp for a couple of days, and I had a few hours to write. At the car garage, I had spoken with the mechanic about chassis and suspensions. As I drove home, I needed to hear another kind of language that would spark my writing that day. Fitzgerald's words did the trick.

Students need to hear the language of words that will inspire them, too. If students are writing narrative, for example, they need to listen to and read quality narrative that will tune their ears and sharpen their crafting tools. If they are writing persuasive essays, they need to marinate in quality persuasive essays.

Sometimes when I'm in the middle of writing, and I feel like I'm slogging through and the words just aren't flowing, I choose a book that I know will sing with my own voice and help me write what I want to.

Students need the same kind of mentors in books and texts. During writing workshop time, I gather some of my favorite books for students on a table, depending on what they're writing: informative and explanatory texts if they're writing informative and explanatory pieces, narrative if they're writing narrative, and so on. I tell them that as they're writing, they should at some point pick up one of these books to see if they can gather any ideas or inspiration from another author's words.

For example, if a student is writing an essay but isn't sure how to begin, she can read how other writers have started their writing and try one of their techniques.

Listening to F. Scott Fitzgerald after running errands gave me the energy and persistence to keep writing and rewriting. When I read or listen to words that stimulate my inner voice, I say, "I can write like that."

Collecting a handful of mentor books, and keeping them as a resource for students, is really like gathering a multitude of teachers in the room rather than having just one teacher.

One way to approach a study of mentor texts is to help your students learn to read like writers. Learning to read with writers' eyes is a way for students to learn craft from authors whom they admire. Teach them to find places in a text that move them, or that they admire, and try to name specifically what that author is doing. Ask them to begin collecting examples of writing that they admire in mentor text notebooks (see my 2013 book *Finding the Heart of Nonfiction: Teaching 7 Essential Craft Tools with Mentor Texts*). These are small notebooks that students use to gather examples of quality writing from their mentor texts. Students might decide to use the same craftsmanship to create similar effects in their own writing.

Self-Assessing

Part of learning to read our writing deeply in preparation for revision is learning to self-assess our writing. Many young writers will not be in the practice of rereading and assessing their own writing. This is a skill that writers learn slowly and over time. The more students practice stopping, rereading, and asking themselves questions about how their writing is going so far, the better they will get at it.

Here is a strategy students can try to begin assessing their writing for the possibilities of revision.

Have two differently colored pens handy. Ask a student to reread a draft of his writing, paying attention to his thinking as he reads. Ask him to underline or mark the words, phrases, and sentences that he thinks are his best writing in one color ink. He might highlight specific words, surprising similes or metaphors, vivid descriptions, or well-said ideas.

Then as he rereads, he should also pay attention to any thoughts or feelings or parts of his writing that he thinks need work, or aren't exactly what he wants to say or how he wants to say it. These could be places that are abstract, words that are vague or cliché, beginnings that need more life, or endings that don't conclude. Ask the writer to mark these parts with the other color.

Afterward, the writer can get together with his writing partner and reflect on what he noticed. The parts he marked as needing improvement will be the places that need revision, and the best writing can be a model for how he wants the rest of the writing to be.

In the beginning, students might find only one word or sentence that needs improvement in their texts. But over time students will be more able to assess their own writing for revision possibilities.

Teachers can model this process first with the whole group, showing how we know when something needs improvement.

For me, revision is a matter of rewriting until what I write feels truthful, complete, and alive. I constantly match what's in my heart and my mind with the words I've written on paper until the match is as perfect as I can make it. Sometimes my writing feels too flat or abstract. Sometimes just tweaking a few words here and there will do it. And sometimes putting a piece of writing away for several days or a week allows me to know what to revise when I take it out again.

I ask students to reread their writing and be honest with themselves about how they really feel. Ask them to measure what's in their hearts or their minds with that they've written. They might ask:

> Where does the writing match what I really want to say?
>
> Where does the writing not match? Why, how, and where do the parts feel not quite right? What is my vision of how my writing would read if it were exactly as I imagined?

Asking ourselves these difficult questions is the core of revision.

Paying Attention to That Sinking Feeling

One of my writing teachers said that the sinking feeling that a writer gets after she reads her piece of writing and realizes that it's not quite right is actually a feeling to be treasured. Why? Because this disappointed feeling means that we have a vision of how we want our writing to be. Many students ball up their papers and throw them in the trash when they realize that their writing isn't what they hoped for. They feel discouraged and don't know how to move forward. We need to teach our students to pay attention to and respect this feeling of disappointment and know that this is often the beginning of the revision process. If they can then pinpoint where they feel the writing goes wrong and where it feels right for them, that's the first step in the process.

Conducting Effective Revision Conferences

In classrooms around the country, the students themselves have helped me learn to revise my conferences with them. I can tell how well I'm doing by their faces, their body language, and, ultimately, their enthusiasm for writing. I'd like to share four conference fundamentals that I've learned about having a positive, constructive conference with students:

1. **Don't be tempted to revise a piece of writing for a student.** It's easy for me to know exactly how to rewrite a student's writing for her. I have years of experience and I'm objective, so why not just mark the paper up with all the changes I think she should make? But what would this teach her? Not much. It would create a dependency on me and a belief that I know better how to revise the students' writing than they do. Instead, I can use my experience and my objectivity to help a writer select one part of her writing to revise so she can gradually feel successful with revision. Although this method is much slower, it will eventually help students take charge of their own revision processes.

2. **It's not necessary to confer with every single student every single day.** Besides being impossible and impractical, we don't need to have a conference with every student every single day. Why? Because change happens slowly. When I confer with a student and suggest a revision strategy to try, I need to give her time to practice. Plus, revision usually happens over time. We can't expect students to revise every piece that they write until it's perfect.

3. **Include students in the "world of writers" by the language you use in a conference.** If we use words of authority ("I think you should add more detail" or "Rewrite the end"), students might try to do what we ask, but they probably won't internalize the revision strategy for themselves. If we call students *writers* and really mean it, we will empower them and invite them into the larger world of writing. I have found that this one, seemingly minor, conferring technique gives students the sense of empowerment to want to revise.

   Here is an example of what I might say in a conference where I am trying to include a student in the world of writers and writing:

   > Many *writers* do exactly what you've done: they write their first thoughts down on paper, but then they realize they have more to say. I'm going to read your writing back to you, and I'd like you to listen and see if there are other images or details that you think you've left out. Just like other *writers* have done, see if you can add these to your writing.

4. **Trust the writer.** I think trusting the writer is the hardest part about being a writing teacher. Allowing my students to make mistakes and stumble around not knowing what they're doing is difficult for me. But I have to remember that writing and revision are messy; they never happen in a neat, packaged, linear way.

And ultimately, I have to trust that every writer has a vision of his own writing—that he knows what he needs to say and how he can say it—and it's my job to guide him toward this vision. Trying not to write the piece of writing for the student according to my vision, letting him discover his own way—this is what responding to a student's writing is all about. It's the biggest challenge we have as teachers.

At the end of every chapter, I've included several examples of strategic conferences specific to the craft tools and ideas discussed in each chapter.

Deep Reading Strategic Conferences

The conferences in this section are typical conferences that occur when students are revising their texts and will help you teach students how to use deep reading to revise effectively.

If You Find . . .

A student has finished writing a draft and doesn't know what to do next:

- ▸ Suggest that she reread the draft with a particular lens, or ask her which lens makes the most sense with which to reread.

A student has trouble knowing what and where to revise:

- ▸ Read the draft out loud to him, or suggest that a writing partner read the draft out loud, and then ask him to listen to hear where he might revise.
- ▸ Suggest that he put the draft away for a day and reread it first thing the next day.

A student has made some revisions and you'd like to find out what they are:

- ▸ Ask her, "What did you revise today? What did you change? How has it made a difference in your writing?"

A student has revised by deleting small words such as *and* and *but*, yet the draft has no focus:

- ▸ Discuss with the student the difference between small- and large-scale revision and ask the student to make a web of her writing to clarify what the focus of her piece is. (See Chapter 5, pages 40 and 43 for more about finding focus and webbing.)

Deep Reading Revision Checklist

❏ Does my draft need large-scale revisions (reseeing, rewriting, or rearranging major parts)?

❏ Have I tried getting perspective on my writing so I'll know what to revise by using one of the two strategies: asking a partner or teacher to read my draft out loud to me (or reading out loud to myself) or putting my writing away for a day?

❏ Does my draft need small-scale revisions (adding or deleting words, sentence combining, etc.)?

❏ Do I frequently use front-end revision by stopping while I'm writing and rereading instead of waiting until I'm finished writing the entire draft?

❏ Which revision lens can I use to reread and revise my draft?

_____

_____

❏ When I have read my draft, and I have found something I don't like, have I gone back to highlight the places that I can revise?

CHAPTER 4

Revision Toolboxes

It was a hot, stifling day in an elementary school in Brooklyn. Although all the windows were as wide-open as possible, no breeze stirred the air. The students and I were gathered on the floor in a fourth-grade classroom. I was talking to these young writers about revising—particularly about drafting. I told them what a draft was and showed them some of my drafts and the changes I made on each one. I told them that each time I revised my writing, I usually began a new draft.

This was my first visit to this classroom, and I could tell that these students were eager to learn and even more eager to try this new writing technique. A few minutes later, the students walked back to their desks and began to write. I was looking forward to seeing what revisions they would make.

They were all diligently writing away. I sat next to Melissa, a soft-spoken girl who liked to write but seldom said a word. I asked her if I could read her writing. She was in the middle of the second draft of her three-page story about her grandfather. As I read her second draft and compared it with the first, I realized that the two drafts were exactly the same.

"Melissa," I asked, "I see you're writing a second draft of your story, but I don't see any of the changes you made from your first to your second. Can you show me where the changes are that you made to your story?"

Melissa pointed to the word *pretty* on the first page, which she had changed from *beautiful* in the first draft, and then she pointed to *and* at the beginning of a sentence in the first draft, which she had cut out in the second. Except for those two words, the drafts were identical.

"Melissa, I'm wondering why you didn't just cross out the words on the first draft instead of copying the whole story over again?"

"Because I thought that's what we were supposed to do."

By the end of the writing workshop period, I noticed that most of the students had written several drafts of stories with only a few words changed. Their folders were becoming filled with papers that had very few revisions.

"Where did I go wrong?" I asked myself as I took the subway back to my apartment later that afternoon.

It wasn't until a few classes later that I understood what had happened that day. The students had done precisely what I had asked. They had changed their writing—a word or two here and there—and for each change, they had written a new draft. The real problem was that these young writers didn't know how or what to change in their writing. I hadn't taught them any specific revision strategies or showed them any examples of revision. I hadn't marinated them in mentor texts so that they could each develop an ear for what good writing sounds like. They had done the best they could do with the knowledge they'd had.

That's when I learned that instead of teaching the concept of *drafts*, I needed to teach concrete revision strategies that students could put in their revision toolboxes. Nowadays, when I introduce revision, I don't even mention the word *draft* until after my students have confidence as writers and a little more experience with revision.

The following three Revision Toolbox chapters discuss a variety of tools that students can put in their toolboxes. A Revision Toolbox filled with an abundance of specific and practical tools will give our students choice when it comes to revising.

I've divided the Revision Toolboxes into three categories: Structure, Words, and Voice. Under each category, I've included an introduction to the toolbox that can be applied to any writing genre, but I've also added subsections that specifically address revision in the three genres emphasized in the Common Core State Standards: persuasive and opinion writing; informative or explanatory writing; and narrative writing.

CHAPTER 5

Revision Toolbox

Structure

[Writing] . . . is a piece of architecture. . . . It's a building—it has to have walls and floors and the bathrooms have to work.

—John Irving

Writing a book, or writing anything (article, essay, etc.), has always reminded me of building a house, and I believe it takes the same amount of patience and planning. Writers organize writing so readers will be invited to enter, get comfortable, and linger awhile. But there's a big difference between writing and building a house: revision. A builder pours the concrete for the foundation and erects the wooden studs, and, eventually, step-by-step a house is built. Not true for writers. Sometimes we need to redo the entire foundation or completely rearrange the walls when we build our "word houses." And in this rewriting and redoing, our essays, articles, poems, and stories are eventually built.

We can help students become more aware of structure by

▸ reading and providing excellent examples of a variety of genres, and identifying and discussing what some of the defining organizational structures might be for each genre;

- ▸ providing planning strategies for students before and during writing drafts; and
- ▸ teaching students organizational strategies and structures for specific genres.

I use the word *structure* for this Revision Toolbox to mean those tools that have to do with planning, rearranging, and organizing a text. The structure of a piece of writing includes a plan for the organization; a focus; the arrangement of text; the introduction or lead and the conclusion; and even organizational units such as paragraphs and chapters.

Planning Your Writing: Rehearsing Orally

When a student spends days, or sometimes weeks, researching and collecting information on a topic or reading a novel, and she feels that she knows her subject well and is ready to write a draft, it's often helpful to talk her writing out prior to drafting. The writer can tell someone what she wants to say in her own words off the top of her head. In this oral rehearsal, an organizational structure sometimes emerges. Sharing our ideas with a partner demands us to focus and organize our thoughts.

Revision Lesson: Thinking Out Loud

When students are ready to write, prior to sharing their ideas out loud students can ask themselves:

What is the focus of my piece?

What is the thesis?

What are some key points?

What has struck me as significant or important to include?

How will I organize and present this information?

Then they can get together in pairs and take turns talking out their writing ideas and how they will write their drafts. They can summarize what their essays or topics are about in their own words. Their partners can take notes, or writers can make outlines of any ideas or ways to organize that are emerging.

Partners might respond or ask:

I heard that the focus of your piece is _____.

(For a longer piece) If you were going to create a table of contents, what would some of the chapter titles be?

(For a shorter piece) What are some of your key points?

If you were going to use one of the structure templates (found on pages 50–52), which one would be most helpful to use?

Revising to Find a Focus

In my book *Finding the Heart of Nonfiction: Teaching 7 Essential Craft Tools with Mentor Texts* (2013), I begin the discussion of nonfiction craft tools with the tool of focus. I love the idea that the word *focus* didn't originally relate to a camera but instead was the Latin word for *hearth*, a place in the home where family and friends come together to warm and comfort themselves. And so with writing, if a piece doesn't have focus, it can seem vague. Writers spend a lot of time making sure that their writing has a focus that's not too general nor too narrow and specific. It's the first task of organizing a piece of writing.

Revision Lesson: Finding Focus in Informative or Explanatory Writing

After a student writes a draft, he can test the chosen focus of his piece by seeing if he can write a title based on the information in the draft. For example, if the student has written an informational piece about jellyfish, and he thinks a fitting title might be "All About Jellyfish," he'll most likely need to rethink and revise by narrowing his topic down, which might necessitate further research. He can ask, "What is it I find the most interesting about jellyfish? Is there an overarching theme or key point that I'd like my readers to know and understand?"

In *Stung! On Jellyfish Blooms and the Future of the Ocean*, by Lisa-ann Gershwin (2013), the focus is not all about jellyfish but instead the very real possibility of jellyfish taking over our oceans in the future because of their ability to adapt and survive where other sea creatures cannot. Every paragraph and example in *Stung!* flows out from that central focus, or *hearth*, and unites the book.

Revision Lesson: Finding Focus in Persuasive or Opinion Essays

I remind my students that, most of the time, the first draft of an essay will not have a clear thesis statement or focus in the beginning. Many times, a thesis emerges only after drafting; it is in the writing that a main idea or thesis becomes clear. Ask students to write fast drafts of their thinking, then reread and highlight possible main points and possible thesis statements.

Revision Lesson: Finding and Elaborating the Heart of a Narrative

Originally, I created the idea of heart mapping as a way for students to find meaningful ideas for writing poems. But I've also used heart mapping to help students focus their narratives, essays, and even informative and explanatory pieces. Raymond Carver wrote, "Maybe I revise because it gradually takes me into the heart of what the story is about. I keep trying to see if I can find that out" (1989).

One question writers often ask themselves, particularly when writing narratives or essays, is, "What is the heart of my piece of writing?" It's similar to the question, "What's my focus?" but it refers not so much to the theme of the writing as to the experience or idea that is central to the writer's emotions and passions about this topic. A concrete way for a student to explore the heart of a text is to draw a heart and then write inside it what the student thinks is at the core of the writing, either before, during, or after writing a draft.

John had written a narrative draft about his grandfather passing away. His first draft was an outline of how his grandfather died, but it didn't seem to get at the heart of his story or his experience. When I met with him in a conference, I asked if he might like to try mapping out his feelings on a heart map to see if it would help him express what he felt about his grandfather's passing. Here John created a heart map in Figure 5–1.

John was able to express his feelings about his grandfather on the heart map and, in the process, find the heart of his narrative, which informed the revision of his piece.

In another example, fifth graders were creating timelines of their personal narratives. To help them revise, I asked each student to draw a heart next to the part, or parts, on the timeline that was the most important part—the heart—of the story. Charlie drew a heart next to *jumping off the diving board* (see Figure 5–2).

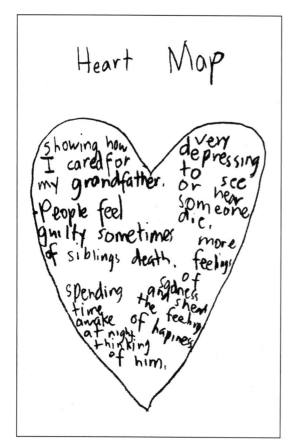

Figure 5–1 John's Heart Map

Figure 5–2 Charlie's Timeline

After identifying the heart of his time-line, Charlie cracked open the important part and elaborated by slowing down the action minute-by-minute and by expanding details (see Figure 5–3).

After a student chooses an important part of her narrative, she can use several re-vision strategies to elaborate:

- slow down the part minute-by-minute (see page 55 for more on slowing down . . . time . . . minute-by-minute)
- add details
- add dialogue

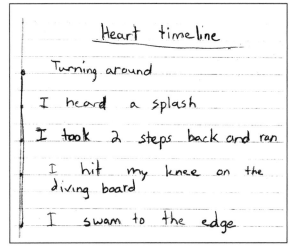

Figure 5–3 Charlie's Heart Timeline

Webbing

Webbing is a focusing tool that I use both before I write and then again after I've written a first draft. When I first begin a piece of writing, I might make a web to explore and expand the many different ideas within one topic. I also make a web after I've already written a draft to help me understand what I've written and to help me organize my thoughts.

Planning a piece of writing requires you to stand back and take a wide, lay-of-the-land view—to see the *gesture* (or essence), as in art classes. Whether you're writing a literary essay, an informative piece, an article, or a narrative, every genre requires focus, organization, and structure.

Leo was assigned to write a literary essay about the book *The Alchemist*, by Paulo Coelho (2006). Although he loved the book, the idea of writing an essay about it was daunting. He asked, "How do I choose what to write about? What's the overarching idea I want to write about?"

Leo's first draft had no organization at all. It was random thoughts. Then his teacher asked him to web his ideas. By webbing, he had to reflect on what was the central idea of the book for him. He liked the idea that the plot of the book is the journey of the main character, Santiago, to find a treasure at the Egyptian pyramids. But he also realized that Santiago's journey to find treasure is a plot device to show his spiritual growth and psychological transformation. He webbed his ideas in three steps. First, he wrote his main idea in the middle of the web. He then wrote his supporting ideas around the central idea. Finally, he reread and found quotes that supported his ideas. After webbing, he was able to more easily write his paper using the web as his blueprint for the structure and paragraphs of his paper (see Figure 5–4).

Webbing can help writers organize writing in a number of ways. Webbing can help writers

- organize and clarify thoughts
- focus on what the most important parts of a piece of writing are
- become aware of a multitude of ideas
- create paragraphs
- create separate chapters and subchapters for longer writing projects

Revision Lesson: Creating a Web

When a student first begins a piece of writing, ask him to create a web and write his topic in the middle of the web and then brainstorm possible ideas around the main topic. (Or students can use the Webbing Template in Appendix D, page 121.)

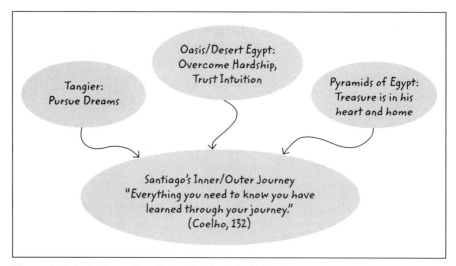

Figure 5–4 Leo's Literary Essay Web of Paul Coelho's *Alchemist*

For many struggling writers, creating a web is a concrete and visual way to help organize their thoughts, extend their writing, and find what's at the center of a piece of writing.

Constructing a Blueprint

In my college drawing class, much of our class time consisted of making gesture drawings. A gesture drawing is usually done quickly, and the purpose is to capture the *essence* or *gesture* of a subject, rather than the minute details. Most art schools use the gesture drawing strategy because it teaches students to see the big picture—the essentials of a figure (the angle of an arm, the tilt of the head, the curve of the back)—rather than the details (a strand of hair, eyelashes or eyebrows on a face, fingernails on fingers, etc.). An artist can render a perfect detail such as an eyelash or eyebrow, but if the structure of the face or the eye isn't there, the details won't make any sense.

With writing it's similar. Writers begin with the big picture—an outline or a plan of how writing will be organized. (Not always, of course; there are times when writers don't start with a plan or an outline, and in the writing process they discover the structure.) It's important to note that an initial plan or outline will most likely be revised during the writing process, but there has to be some structure. For no matter how beautiful or concise your prose is, if your writing doesn't have a focus or an organizational structure that lays out your story or ideas logically, clearly, and purposefully, the reader won't be able to follow it.

Ken Follett said:

> Everything is planned. I spent a long time outlining. It's the only way I know to get all the ducks in a row. . . . The research is the easiest. The outline is the most fun because you can do anything. The first draft is the hardest, because every word of the outline has to be fleshed out. The rewrite is very satisfying, because I feel that everything I do is making the book a little better. (2002)

Every writing genre has its own inherent structure: poetry's organizational units are lines and stanzas and, in the case of formal poetry, meter and set forms; narrative usually follows the arc of a story with a character's problem and resolution; an essay often has a thesis or main point followed by detailed points and examples to support this thesis; informative and explanatory writing often begin by introducing a topic clearly, then developing the topic with definitions, concrete details, quotations, and other information, grouping and organizing related information into broad categories and subcategories.

The following are several organizational tools and templates students can use when revising the structure of their texts. I suggest that students write their first drafts and then read what they have written with the lens of structure and organization. If a student finds that there is no structure in her draft, then she might want to use an outline to fill in any structural holes or to help organize her thinking. You want to make sure that students don't begin with an outline that could constrict their writing.

Revision Lesson: Building a Story Mountain for Narrative Writing

Oftentimes students finish narrative drafts and declare, "I'm done!" Many first drafts of stories include vivid details, but revision often demands a re-seeing of the narrative structure. Reseeing the structure of their narratives gives students a chance to reimagine their stories and shift ideas and characters in large-scale ways. The way writers organize narrative writing is very different from the structure of explanatory essays. Students can study the structure of narrative mentor texts and notice that many narratives use the same basic structure:

- ▸ main character
- ▸ problem
- ▸ details and experiences related to problem
- ▸ resolution

Students might want to use story maps to map out their narrative structures, like the one in Figure 5–5 (see also Appendix E, page 122).

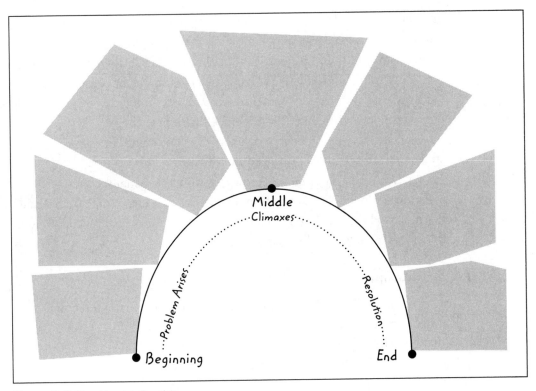

Figure 5–5 Story Mountain Template

Revision Lesson: Creating a Template for Opinion or Persuasive Writing

When I attended a lecture by Tony Wagner, author of *Creating Innovators* (2012), he reminded me of something I've known for a while—that writing is thinking. He said that when he interviewed several CEOs of successful companies, one of the qualities they said was absent from many job applicants was the ability to write. But he said in his lecture we know that a lack of clear writing skills is often a reflection of the absence of clear thinking.

When I write essays I rarely begin with an outline or a preplanned structure. As I write, and my thinking becomes clearer, my essay becomes more organized—my thoughts dictate the structure. I'm not a proponent of the three- to five-paragraph essay because it can become prescriptive and formulaic, and students frequently end up filling in the outline instead of freewriting, exploring, and learning to think more deeply about a topic. However, many students might need the extra support that a blueprint or outline can give them, especially after they've written their first drafts, as long as it helps guide their thinking. Teachers might offer this outline to students after they freewrite, web, or write drafts, and only as a way to help them develop their ideas. If it becomes restrictive, then I tell students to abandon the outline. Teachers can also direct students to mentor texts to study how other authors organized their writing.

It's helpful to let students know that an essay usually pivots around a main idea or thesis and to clarify and write out on a chart some of the qualities of a good thesis. When students are revising, they might want to check this thesis guideline and revise accordingly.

A Good Thesis . . .

- makes a claim about something that needs to be supported and/or something you're going to argue
- can be defined, explained, and supported
- is usually placed in the introductory paragraph

Students might want to use webbing as a way to explore a thesis and supporting evidence, or some students might prefer a more linear template like the one in Figure 5–6. The structure of an essay might go something like that figure shows (see also Appendix F, page 123).

Revision Lesson: Creating a Template for Informative or Explanatory Writing

The structure of an informative or explanatory text can be varied depending on the topic and the purpose of the text. After students have gathered, reread, and organized their thinking and their notes on a topic, they must decide how best to present the information to the reader. Students can use a web to chunk information and place facts into broad categories that will become paragraphs and, with larger amounts of information, chapters.

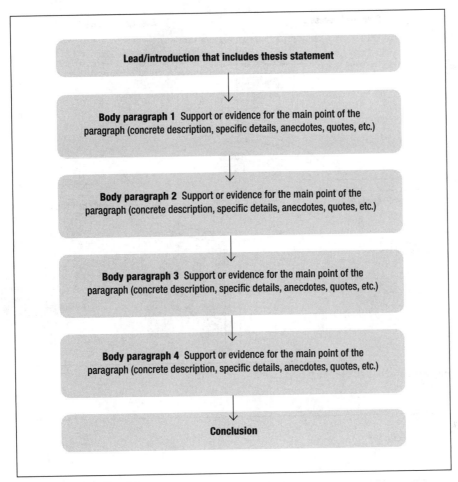

Figure 5–6 Essay Template

They can also use one of the informative or explanatory templates to help clarify their ideas. As with the essay template, teachers should be mindful when giving templates to students that students don't feel they need to "fill in the blanks" and feel inhibited by the structures. Rather, after freewriting or orally rehearsing a draft, a student might use one of the five templates shown in Figures 5–7 through 5–11 to help revise and develop the ideas (see also Appendixes G through K, pages 124–128, respectively).

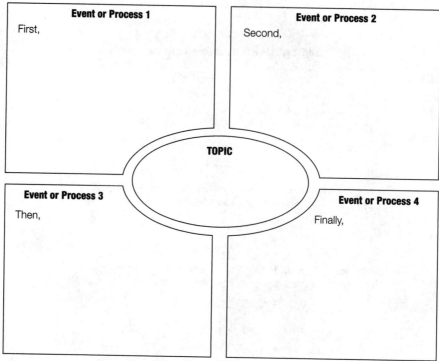

Figure 5–7 Sequence Template

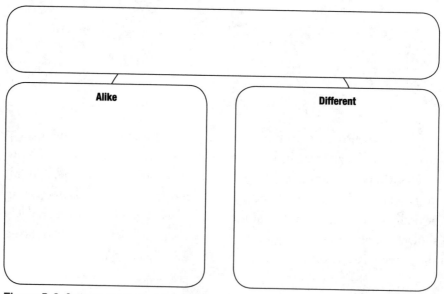

Figure 5–8 Compare-and-Contrast Template

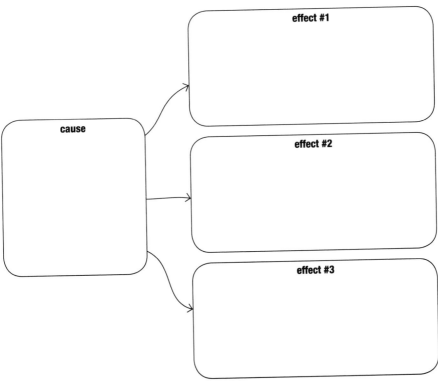

Figure 5–9 Cause-and-Effect Template

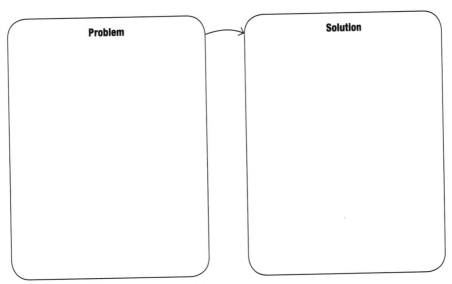

Figure 5–10 Problem-and-Solution Template

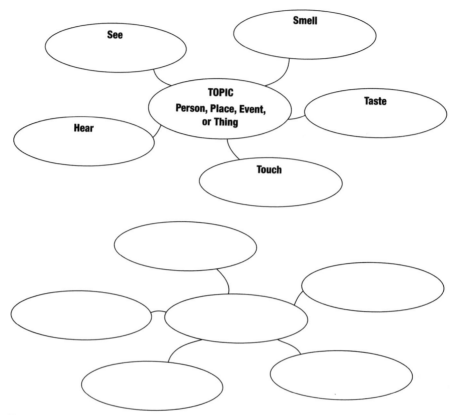

Figure 5–11 Description Template

Revising Toward Unity

When a student has found her focus and found a possible structure for her piece, she might need to revise to make sure that every fact, quote, and piece of information contributes to the unity or focus of the piece. Every sentence and paragraph should add to the main point, topic, or thesis the writer wants to make.

Revision Lesson: Checking for Consistency

As a student rereads a draft, he can highlight, or point out with a finger, the main idea or key point in each paragraph. He can reread and cut out any unnecessary facts that don't contribute to the focus of the piece and disrupts the unity and flow. He can also create a web as he rereads, checking to make sure that all the information promotes the main idea, topic, or thesis.

As he rereads, the writer can ask himself:

Does each bit of information develop my main thesis statement or reason?

Is each bit of information different and distinct, or do some of them overlap?

Organizing a Parade of Actions, Facts, and Ideas

Sometimes when I think back over my life, I can see it like a movie—a parade of actions (my own and other people's), one after another. Some of these actions are big and significant, like when I got married or gave birth to my son, and other actions are small and seemingly minor, like when I broke my favorite coffee mug. We can build our stories, essays, and informative pieces in the same way—action by action, scene by scene, evidence by evidence, fact by fact. Thinking of writing in this way helps us think in local rather than universal terms.

Following are three essentials you may want to discuss with your students about writing narrative scenes.

Writing Scenes in Narratives

1. A scene has a setting or a specific location that the reader can picture. You want to be sure to draw your readers into the world you've created—to make them feel like it's their world and forget where they are for the moment.
2. A scene is composed of an action—something that happens. This will give your writing a sense of immediacy.
3. Apply the old truism *show, don't tell* to the writing of scenes: don't tell the reader about the action; take her there.

Following are three essentials you may want to discuss with your students about writing facts, information, or ideas in an informative or explanatory piece.

Writing Facts in Informative or Explanatory Texts

1. Create a new paragraph or section for each new fact or idea.
2. *Show* us a fact by describing—creating an image or a scene— instead of just *telling* us a fact.
3. Group similar facts or bits of information into chapters and subheadings.

Following are three essentials you may want to discuss with your students about writing ideas and thoughts in opinion or persuasive writing.

Writing Ideas in Opinion or Persuasive Pieces

1. Show evidence to support each new idea or thought.
2. Build each new idea or thought in a new paragraph.
3. Move your finger down the page, pointing to and counting each new idea or thought. This will help students self-assess, assuring that each point is new and not overlapping with another, as well as clarify what each new idea or thought is.

Playing with Time

One of the most powerful tools available to any writer is being able to play with time. We can begin at the end of a story and go back to the beginning, and jump all around a day, a year, even a life.

Revision Lessons: Strategies for Revising Time

Ask students to make timelines of their narratives. You might want to give them sentence strips or adding machine tape as material for creating timelines. To practice making timelines, students can create timelines of books they already know. Picture books are a good place to start because they're short and easy to map out.

Next, ask each student to select a narrative he's written and create a timeline of the big events and actions, paying particular attention to the elements of time such as what happened at the beginning, how much time passed between the big events and actions, and how the narrative ends.

Flashback

One of the revision strategies that I frequently introduce to students is flashback. On their timelines, if their stories are chronological, ask them to try beginning their stories at the end of their timelines, and flash back to the beginning to see how this new way of structuring time transforms their stories.

Slow Motion

One of my favorite parts of watching a sport on television, whether it's tennis, basketball, skating, or skiing, is the replay. After a spectacular play, jump, or spin, the television replays it in slow motion so that viewers can see just how spectacular it was in full slowed-down details: we can see again how perfect the landing was on the triple flip or what an incredible serve it was, but this time in slow motion.

Good writing is filled with these slowed-down moments where we can fully live the details of a story, poem, or memoir. Writers slow time down by focusing on details, painting vivid scenes and images, and including dialogue.

Ask each student to place a heart or circle on a part of her narrative on the timeline that feels like an important part. On another piece of paper, the student should expand that part by slowing down time and including details as if it were happening in slow motion. (See Charlie's timeline in Figure 5–3.)

Big Sweeps of Time

Another playing-with-time revision strategy is to speed time up. Many beginning writers think they must tell a detailed account of every moment and hour of the day. A good piece of writing usually includes both expanded moments as well as big sweeps of time where days, months, and even years are condensed to a sentence or two.

One of Allison Sekol's seventh-grade students, Abby, used this "big sweep of time" strategy in her story about her trip to Sao Paulo, Brazil, to see her father: "Seven days, a sunburn and a couple of lizards that I could have done without. It was time to begin the end of our journey."

Ask each student to identify places on a narrative timeline where the student can condense time, so that not every moment of the narrative will be equally detailed.

Opening the Front Door: The Lead or Introduction

When you open the front door of a house and step inside, you can sense immediately if you're comfortable or even if you want to stay awhile. With just a quick glance around, you can get a feel for the people who live in the house.

Similarly, the lead or introduction to a piece of writing is the "front door." You want your guests or readers to feel compelled to stay and linger. For the writer, the lead can be like a catalyst to push the rest of the writing along, as John McPhee says:

> Once I've written the lead, I read the notes and then
> I read them again. . . . Ideas occur, but what I'm
> doing, basically is looking for logical ways in which
> to subdivide the materials. I'm looking for things
> that fit together, things that can relate. (2012)

The following are a few types of front doors, or ways to open a piece of writing. In my book *Finding the Heart of Nonfiction: Teaching 7 Essential Craft Tools with Mentor Texts* (2013), you'll find many more examples of nonfiction leads.

QUESTION Many writers begin with a question. What's more compelling than a question that begs to be answered?

DIALOGUE Dialogue pulls the reader into the piece. When the reader walks through this door, she is forced to engage in the story because she's stepping right into the middle of the action, as in this example from *The Watcher: Jane Goodall's Life with the Chimps*, by Jeanette Winter.

> "Jane, Jane, where are you?"
> "Jane, can you hear me?"
> EVERYONE had been searching for hours and hours,
> looking for little Valerie Jane Goodall.
> Then, from the henhouse,
> Jane came running to her mother, shouting—
> "I know how an egg comes out!"
> At five years old, Jane was already a watcher. (2011)

INTERESTING FACT A writer might want to grab his reader with an interesting fact when the reader first opens the door. This is a sure way to capture the reader's attention. Ask your students to scan the articles in a newspaper and make a survey of what type of lead sentences the articles begin with. Many articles begin with an interesting fact or a surprising statement that will get the reader's attention. For example:

> Frogs are found on every continent except Antarctica. They live in ponds, rivers, forests, and fields. Some even live in sand dunes. (Bishop 2008, 5)

IMAGE An image paints an immediate picture and creates a world that the reader can step into. In Richard's narrative about sailing in Maine, his lead paints a vivid picture in our minds and compels us to read on (see Figure 5–12).

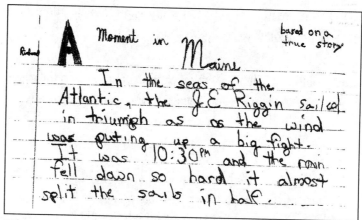

Figure 5–12 Richard's Great Lead

> *In the seas of the Atlantic, the J. E. Riggin sailed*
> *in triumph as the wind was putting up a big fight.*
> *It was 10:30 p.m. and the rain fell down so hard*
> *it almost split the sails in half.*

COMPELLING THOUGHT OR IDEA A student might want to open an essay with a thought or an idea that will compel the reader to read on.

> If you look at zero you see nothing; but look
> through it and you will see the world. (Kaplan
> 1999, 1)

QUOTATION Many literary essays begin with poignant quotes from books that hint at what the theses will be.

Revision Lesson: Writing Compelling Leads

Here are three suggestions you can give to students for revising leads:

1. Oftentimes a good lead is buried right in the narrative, essay, or informative or explanatory piece itself. Ask your students to reread a piece of writing and underline a sentence or part that might serve as a compelling lead.

2. Ask your students to write three or four alternative leads before they choose the one they'll finally use in their piece of writing.

3. Ralph Fletcher, the wonderful author of *Mentor Author, Mentor Texts* (2011) as well as many other books on writing, uses a beautiful metaphor to describe the process of revising the lead: writing as a waterfall. He says that many beginning writers start their pieces too far up the stream, away from the roar of the waterfall. When a writer searches for a lead, he should always begin at the roar of the waterfall, at an engaging place, and start his piece of writing there. The writer should cut the rest of the writing that meanders slowly toward the roar.

Rearranging the Furniture: Cutting and Taping

If writing is a house, or even a room in a house, then the cut-and-tape revision strategy is akin to rearranging the furniture. Sometimes writers are wedded to the way their words are first written—both the meaning and the order they wrote them in. This revision strategy can help writers in two ways.

First, by highlighting and "chunking" the various parts or ideas of a piece of writing, a student can cut the highlighted parts and rearrange them. By doing this, the student might discover a new way to begin or end or a new way to tell the story or organize the ideas.

Second, if a student wants to revise by adding more description or detail to a text, instead of copying over the entire piece, the student can simply cut the writing apart, leaving space to add the new details, and then tape the original writing to the new material.

I have found this revision strategy works well if students understand the concept of adding details and elaborating first. I've been in many classes where I've introduced the cut-and-tape revision strategy, and the novelty of using scissors and tape was the focus rather than revision.

If students are writing on computers, then they can cut and paste easily. It's important, however, for students to keep copies of their drafts prior to cutting and pasting, so if they decide they prefer to keep their original drafts they can return to them.

Revision Lesson: Rearranging Words

Ask each student to select a piece of writing or notebook passage to revise. Ask the student to make a copy of the writing so the student doesn't have to worry about cutting the writing up and not knowing how to put it back the way he wrote it.

The student should then highlight or put brackets around the main parts of the writing (if it's written in paragraphs, this will be easier to do) and then cut each highlighted or bracketed part out with scissors. Next, the writer can rearrange the parts: move the end to the beginning; a middle section to the beginning; the beginning to the end; and so on. This is the writer's chance to play, rearrange, and experiment with reorganizing a text to see the possibilities for revision.

Revision Lesson: Adding Details, Evidence, and Facts

Ask each student to select a piece of writing that the student has reread and wants to add more details, evidence, or facts to. Ask the writer to mark with an asterisk where she wants to add more and then cut the writing there. Tell the student to tape the top part of the writing on a blank sheet of paper and write new details in the space below. The student should write the new details first and then tape the bottom portion of the writing beneath that.

Leaving the House: The Ending

At night, when I'm reading a bedtime story to my son and we come to the end of the book, I've gotten into the habit of saying "The End" even if the book doesn't include those words. This gives the story a kind of double closure just in case my son doesn't really know the story is over, and it's time to turn out the light and go to sleep.

I read back over what I wrote here eleven years ago when my son was three, and feelings of nostalgia sweep over me: that that time in my son's life is over, and he is a teen now. And just like with all endings, I am left with lingering memories, feelings, and thoughts. Life is a series of beginnings and endings we face every day, and in writing, a good ending gives us closure and resolution.

The point of ending a piece of writing is to leave something worthwhile for the reader to savor, and depending on the genre, *worthwhile* can mean many different things. For nonfiction, endings often tie things up and create a sense that what the reader read is substantial. A good conclusion also relates back to the core of a narrative or central meaning or theme of any piece of writing. Readers need to feel that there is a resolution to the writing. The end of a piece of writing is more difficult than the beginning to revise because the entire structure of the piece must lead up to the end. You can't just write a huge "The End" to end a piece, as some young writers are tempted to do.

The more students are aware of the various kinds of endings writers use, the more choices they'll have available to them as they write their endings.

Revision Lessons: Creating Satisfying Endings

Each student can reread a piece of writing that he or she has already written and explore one of the following types of endings.

Circular Ending

A circular ending gives a sense of closure and gives writing a beautiful cyclic structure. It also gives your readers a chance to revisit the issue you presented in your writing. Maxine Kumin spoke about this kind of ending as a "snake with a tail in its mouth." Patricia MacLachlan uses a circular ending in her beautiful picture book *Through Grandpa's Eyes* (1980). She uses the line "because I see it through Grandpa's eyes" in the first paragraph and then repeats it as the last line of the book. The entire book is about how a young boy learns to see the beauty in the world through his grandpa's eyes although his grandpa has lost his sight. By the very last line, the reader truly understands the depth of the seeing that the boy's grandpa has taught him.

Circular endings are not only for narratives but can also be used in nonfiction genres. In my book *Finding the Heart of Nonfiction: Teaching 7 Essential Craft Tools with Mentor Texts* (2013), I cite *Surprising Sharks*, by

Nicola Davies (2003), who uses a circular ending that recalls the beginning with a changed message:

Beginning

You're swimming in the warm blue sea. What's the one word that turns your dream into a nightmare? What's the one word that makes you think of a giant man-eating killer? Shaaaaarrrkk! (6)

Ending

If you were a shark swimming in the lovely blue sea, the last word you'd want to hear would be . . . human! (27)

Quotation

Ending an article or essay with a quote drives the point of the writing home through somebody else's expertise or opinion and gives the writing another layer of authority. As I was reading the *New York Times* one morning, I surveyed the endings of articles and found that over half ended with quotations. Readers tend to believe the words of an expert or an authority on a particular subject, especially if that expert has the last word.

Pithy Point

One of my favorite nonfiction endings is a pithy statement that makes reference to something mentioned earlier in the text, ties the point of view or the information together, and even adds a dash of humor. Recently, I read an article in the *Atlantic* magazine titled "How Three Weeks in New Zealand Changed My Relationship with Food: A Journey from Table to Farm." Here's the conclusion:

After traveling 27 hours across the globe and returning to my city-based life, I found myself appreciating my relationship with both the food I eat and the producers who provide it. . . . Even if I

have no immediate plans to be the one plucking
feathers from a chicken with its head cut off.
(Wilson 2013, 43)

There are, of course, many other ending types that students can use.
Here is a list of several more:

- question
- surprise
- chronological conclusion
- emotional statement
- image

Ask your students to study the endings of some of their favorite books or
articles and come up with more categories for ending their writing.

Structure Strategic Conferences

The conferences in this section are typical conferences that occur when students are revising the structure of their texts and will help you teach students how to revise effectively.

If You Find . . .

A student has revised by adding details and elaborating, but the elaboration is not an important part of the piece:

- ▸ Suggest that the writer make a heart map and explore what she thinks the heart of her story or piece is.
- ▸ Suggest that the writer use a web to explore her topic, writing the topic in the center of the web and surrounding that central topic with information that supports the topic.

A student has written a draft of an essay with no focus or thesis statement:

- ▸ Suggest that the writer talk out loud to a partner or to you about what he thinks the important points or main ideas are that could possibly be a focus or thesis statement.
- ▸ Suggest that the student write a flash draft of some of his thinking, then reread and highlight main points for a possible focus and thesis statement.

A student has written a draft with details but no structure:

- ▸ Suggest that the writer use one of the structure templates (depending on the genre) to help structure the writing.

A student has finished a draft but the ending feels chopped off:

- ▸ Suggest that the student freewrite any final thoughts he might have about his ideas.
- ▸ Suggest that the student search for a good quote that will tie up and help resolve the story or ideas.

Structure Revision Checklist

- ❏ Have I found a clear focus? (all genres)

- ❏ Have I found the heart of my story? (narrative)

- ❏ Have I developed a clear thesis statement? (opinion and persuasive writing, or essay)

- ❏ Have I reread to make sure that I'm grouping similar information into paragraphs and sections?

- ❏ Have I reread to make sure that every part of my writing supports my topic, thesis, or main idea?

- ❏ Have I zoomed in on an important part?

- ❏ Do I have a clear and interesting lead or introduction?

- ❏ Do I have a clear ending that resolves my narrative or topic?

- ❏ Have I used a genre structure template to check my structure?

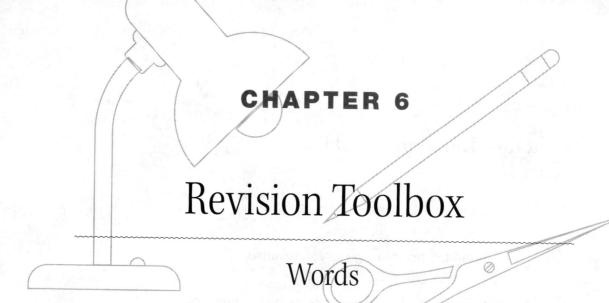

CHAPTER 6

Revision Toolbox

Words

The difference between the almost-right word and the right word is the difference between the lightning bug and the lightning.

—Mark Twain

My computer's screen saver is a word aquarium: words glide like fish across a watery blue screen. Words that I know but seldom use, like *topiary, synchronicity,* and *causerie,* float in front of me. I press a key for more information on *ruction,* a strange-sounding word that I don't know, and read the definition: *a disturbance or quarrel.* "Of course," I say to myself, "like *ruckus.*" These are my small writer's breaks as I sip coffee and ruminate on the word-fish swimming across my screen before I plunge into my own writing project again.

Writers are always navigating the world of language. We have developed a keen awareness, almost a hyperawareness, of the nuances and sounds of words. It is what we do. It gives us pleasure and inspires us.

This Revision Toolbox is fundamental to revision and one way to begin when trying to promote and develop revision in students' language and sentences. The revision lessons in this toolbox will encourage students to revise their writing by exploring, playing with, rearranging, cutting out, and cracking open words. But developing word awareness in our students is more than just an exercise in helping them know which words to cut out—it's about deepening their understanding of and curiosity about language.

Word Treasures: Word Collections

When my husband and I walk on the beach, I frequently stop to pick up sea glass. I have an eye for spotting even the smallest piece of sea glass buried halfway in the sand. In my study where I write, I keep a clear glass bowl on a shelf filled with my sea glass collection. Over six years, the bowl has become filled to the brim with white, green, blue, and brown sea glass that has been tossed by the ocean—hard edges softened by years of burnishing.

Writers collect words the same way that I collect sea glass. The more words we collect in our notebooks, the more words we'll know and have access to when we write. What words we decide to collect is up to each of us, and each writer's collection is different.

I once heard a radio show about language that revealed that the French people's favorite words in the English language are the words *cellar door*. Why? Because they love the sounds of these words.

Roald Dahl writes in his notebook:

> When I began my career as a writer, I started collecting words in an old school notebook. Half of the pages in this book have nothing but lists of words—mostly adjectives and adverbs. When you're describing something or someone, you can't just choose dull words like "beautiful," "pretty," or "nice." You must search for more meaty and imaginative words. Keeping lists, which I can easily refer to, when I'm writing helps me to find the exact word I'm looking for.

Revision Lesson: Gathering Words

Ask students to each begin a collection of words in a notebook or in a special folder. Here are some criteria you can give them for collecting words:

- ▸ words they love the sound of
- ▸ words they don't know the meanings of but would like to find out
- ▸ words they've read in books that look interesting
- ▸ words that give them strong images
- ▸ words that evoke memories
- ▸ domain-specific words on topics they're interested in

Once students have collected their treasure words, they can share their favorites with their partners, discussing why they collected those particular words.

The point of collecting words is not to put them to use right away, but to create awareness that words are treasures meant to be savored.

What Word Revision Looks Like

As an introduction to word revision, particularly to the power that words carry and the profound differences revision can make, I ask students to look at two versions of a text. A good example of revision is the two versions of the last paragraph of Abraham Lincoln's first inaugural address (March 4, 1861). The first version was written by Secretary of State William Henry Seward, and the second version includes Lincoln's brilliant revisions. (For a less difficult example, see revisions of my poem "Dragonfly" in Appendix L, page 129.)

Revision Lesson: Looking at Word Revision

Gather students in a large group or in small partnerships and give them copies of the two versions of Lincoln's speech (see Appendix M, page 132). Ask students to read the two drafts and write down and discuss the differences between Seward's version and Lincoln's revision, paying particular attention to changes in words and sentences. They can then discuss how Lincoln's revisions change the quality of the writing. Seward's version is competent but Lincoln's revision "sharpen[s] Seward's patriotic sentiments into a concise and powerful poetry" (Goodwin 2006, 326).

First, Seward's draft:

> I close. We are not, we must not be, aliens or enemies, but fellow-countrymen and brethren. Although passion has strained our bonds of affection too hardly, they must not, I am sure they will not, be broken. The mystic chords which, proceeding from so many battle-fields and so many patriot graves, pass through all the hearts and all the hearths in this broad continent of ours, will yet again harmonize in their ancient music when breathed upon by the guardian angels of the nation. (Goodwin 2006, 326)

Here is Lincoln's revision:

> I am loath to close. We are not enemies, but friends. We must not be enemies. Though passion may have strained, it must not break our bonds of affection. The mystic chords of memory, stretching from every battle-field and patriot grave to every living heart and hearthstone all over this broad land, will yet swell the chorus of the Union, when again touched, as surely they will be, by the better angels of our nature. (Goodwin 2006, 326)

Following are some of the major changes in the words and sentences that my students have noticed about Lincoln's version:

- ▸ Lincoln's use of the word *loath* in the first sentence shows his deepest feelings of how much he hated the rift between the North and the South, instead of Seward's *I close*, which feels a little empty and void of feeling compared with Lincoln's version.

▸ Lincoln's first few sentences are shorter, more direct, and therefore have more of an emotional impact:

Seward: We are not, we must not be, aliens or enemies . . .

Lincoln: We are not enemies, but friends. We must not be enemies.

You can dig a little deeper and ask students to pinpoint exactly what the difference is between the two versions and why Lincoln's sentences are more powerful than Seward's.

▸ Instead of Seward's "The mystic chords which, proceeding from so many battle-fields and so many patriot graves, pass through all the heart and all the hearths in this broad continent of ours . . . ," Lincoln revised it to "The mystic chords of memory, stretching from every battle-field and patriot grave to every living heart and hearthstone all over this broad land . . ." Lincoln's addition of the word *memory* in "The mystic chords of memory" is brilliant because he defines while Seward only alludes. The word *stretching* is concrete, unlike Seward's *proceeding*, and Lincoln's "living heart and hearthstone" feels more genuine than Seward's "all the heart and all the hearths."

It's the quality of Lincoln's words and the simplicity and variation of his sentences—short sentences juxtaposed against one long sentence toward the end of the paragraph—among other revisions that transform his speech from prosaic to poetic. But *how* do these revisions transform a piece of competent writing into writing that is memorable and deeply moving? How was Lincoln able to revise so expertly? My belief is that Lincoln ran Seward's initial draft through his heart and his mind—meaning that it wasn't just a mental exercise in making the speech a better piece of writing—and grounded his revisions in what he truly felt and believed. In other words, passion and conviction led his revisions.

The words writers choose reflect their thinking, beliefs, and feelings. A boring word or a utilitarian sentence will get its point across but won't move the reader.

Specificity of Words

After school, Leo and I frequently stop by the best frozen yogurt store in town. The store is set up with self-serve machines lined up along the wall. We start from one end of the machines and browse the flavors, stopping to pour small samples in tiny paper cups. One time, Leo had decided on Cable Car Chocolate and I was looking for vanilla. I noticed that there was not just one vanilla but five different kinds. I began taste testing all five. I wanted to know what the difference was between Country Vanilla, Alpine Vanilla, Fancy French Vanilla, White Vanilla, and no-sugar-added vanilla. My mouth salivated when I thought of Country Vanilla, so I started there. As I tasted, I also started ruminating on the specificity of words. Writers can use either plain vanilla words or more specific words that give specific flavors (pun intended). Think about it: What do you think the taste difference is between Country Vanilla and Alpine Vanilla? Just from what the words evoked, I imagined that Country Vanilla would be what we used to call just plain vanilla, and Alpine Vanilla might taste similar but creamier. When I tasted the two, I discovered I was right. Whoever created the yogurt flavors understood the nuances of words.

Leo had already filled his yogurt cup and was now working on adding toppings: mini gummy bears, rainbow sprinkles, and mochi. My thoughts were interrupted by "Are you ready, Mom?" I realized then that I was full. I'd tasted five different flavors of vanilla and I didn't want anymore. I apologized to the salesperson that I was actually not going to get any yogurt and told her that I'd be happy to pay for the yogurt I sampled. She smiled and said it was OK.

Revision is about making choices in our writing. The word choices we make can be general, which won't allow our readers to experience our writing fully, or they can be specific, which will invite our readers into the world of our writing (like the names of the different flavors of vanilla in the yogurt store). We want our readers to feel what we feel, experience what we see, hear, taste, and smell. That's why being specific is crucial to expressing our hearts and minds.

Cracking Open Words: Elaboration

A geode is one of nature's treasures. From the outside it appears to be an ordinary rock, but if you crack it open with a hammer, you'll most likely see a beautiful hidden crystal.

Similarly, writers break apart their words, sentences, and drafts to get to the "crystal" part of their writing. I've called this revision strategy "cracking open words" because the process is similar to cracking a geode open. Words like *fun, nice, pretty, wonderful,* and *scary* are all generic words that don't describe anything specific for the reader or give the reader any particular picture in her mind.

Revision Lesson: Cracking Open Words in Any Genre

You might want to bring a geode into class to make the metaphor of cracking open writing more tangible. (Be sure you have an old sock handy to put your geode in before you smash it; that way the rock pieces will stay contained and won't fly around and hurt someone.)

Start with individual words. Ask your students to help you compile a list of tired, worn, and overused words that they've noticed in their own writing. You'll probably want to begin the list with your own examples of worn words. The criteria I give them for collecting these tired words are as follows:

- vague, abstract words
- clichés
- words or phrases used more than once
- "habit words" (words a writer uses too frequently)

After you've compiled a good class list together, ask students to work independently on their own writing to highlight any words that they think they can flesh out. Then they can share those words in partnerships.

Then students can move to cracking open sentences. You can give your students this list of generic sentences that I have collected from student writing to revise independently or in partnerships:

It was a nice day.

I had a lot of fun.

The flowers were colorful.

Snow is nice.

She is a wonderful person.

Ask your students to each take a metaphoric hammer and crack open these generic sentences. After choosing one particular sentence, a student can place an equal sign next to it, and leave space next to it to write. Then the student should close his eyes and resee, for example, what "a nice day" might look and feel like, and then describe what he sees in his mind using words. Remind your students to use other senses beyond the visual.

The following is an example of Noah's work at cracking open a sentence:

> *It was a nice day.* =

> *The sun came up over the sea. Cold water*
> *splashed my feet sending a chill over my body.*
> *The air smelled of sweet salt water. The sun-*
> *rays made the water glitter like fireworks. The*
> *sand felt warm on my frozen feet. The wet*
> *rocks made a beautiful shade of gray. The stars*
> *came up. The little sparkling dots made me feel*
> *safe in bed.*

The images that this third grader saw in his mind are vivid and concrete and good examples of how writers can sharpen a vague sentence.

After students have tried this strategy on the sample sentences, ask them to try it in their own writing. A student can reread a piece of her own writing, find one word or sentence that she can crack open, and ask herself, "Where can I elaborate? Where can I add more detail?" She can mark the places that need elaborating with asterisks so she'll remember where to add more details.

Patricia Habicht, a teacher in Maryland, introduced the "cracking open words" strategy using the geode image and then asked her eighth graders to select and underline a few ordinary sentences from their narrative writing. One of her students, Kris, originally wrote:

> *It was kind of dark.* =

Here's his revised, cracked-open version:

> *The sun barely peeks through the curtain, making the empty living room dim, not the grim kind of dim, but a serene dim that leads the mind to creativity.*

Monica chose to revise this sentence:

> *My brother Dave, the creative one, went upstairs and got his bin of Legos.* =

Her new version:

> *Suddenly, a smile springs upon his face as he raises a finger in excitement. I'm confident that if you look hard enough you can actually see a light bulb flash above his head. "I've got it!" he yelps. With a bird watcher's blink he is gone. Moments later, he appears in front of me with a large red bin.*

Cracking open even one sentence can change the tone of the entire piece and add concrete description that will help any writing come alive.

Revision Lessons: Elaborating in Narrative Writing

A purpose of narrative writing is to tell a story, and one of the tools narrative writers use is vivid imagery consisting of words that create a clear picture in the reader's mind. After writing a draft, a student can revise his words to make them more vivid and distinct.

Show, Don't Tell

Another way of describing *crack open words* is *show, don't tell*. To teach students how to show, don't tell, ask them each to draw a line down the middle of a piece of paper, dividing it into two sections like a T-chart. First each student should write down a fact, or highlight a *telling* sentence, or an idea, the student has already written, in the upper left-hand section. Next to it, in the right-hand section, the student should *show* a scene, fact, or idea instead of telling about it.

Figure 6–1 shows two examples of fifth-grade students' show, don't tell revisions.

And in her historical narrative "The Parlor," Erica, a fourth grader, wanted to show, not just tell, the kinds of gifts that people in the eighteenth century might have brought when visiting a family in mourning (see Figure 6–2). The narrative is written from the point of view of a girl who is living in the 1700s whose sister has passed away and who is writing in her diary. Note Erica's attempt at writing in a colonial period voice and using words of that period such as *'tis* and *Sister* (see Chapter 7 for more on point of view).

Tell	Show
She was weak and ill.	She couldn't even get out of bed. Her face was white. She had a bowl next to her bed in case she threw up.

Tell	Show
Then she got really mad.	Her face got red and her eyes got red and her lips scrunched. She started hitting, throwing and kicking things.

Figure 6–1 George's and Cindy's Show, Don't Tell Revision T-Charts

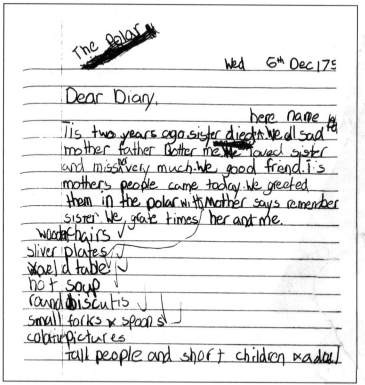

Figure 6–2 "The Parlor," by Erica

Dear Diary,
Tis two years ago sister died (her name was
Polly). We are all sad. Mother, Father, Brother,
Me we loved sister and miss her very much. We
[were] good friends. Mother's people came today.
We greeted them in the parlor with wooden
chairs, silver plates, [the] old table, hot soup,
round biscuits, small forks and spoons, colorful
pictures, tall people and short children and
adults. Mother says remember sister. We [had]
great times her and me.

Figure 6–3 shows Erica's second draft, after she elaborated and added
details and then incorporated them into the piece.

Erica _____

A sad day.   Dec 6 1752

    Tis two years ago sister died her named was Polly. Mother father brother me are sad. We loved sister and missed her very much. Late today mother and father's people will come.
    Tis late today. Me and brother greet people and they tell us "sorry". Me and brother wonder why. After everyone is there we go to polar. The sit at long ovel table with wooden chairs. In front of them sit sliver shinning plates with a fork and spoon on the right. Mother brings in soup and biscuits. People give us all kids of gifts. We ware them. I got a white lovly dress.
    I loved sister very much. Mother said to think are good time. Tis nice we got gifts but I love sister more.

Figure 6–3 "A Sad Day," by Erica

Reseeing to Add Imagery

I gave a minilesson to a class of young writers who were just finishing up writing personal narratives. When I read their narratives, I noticed that many of them were typical first drafts—outlines of stories with few details. When I gathered the class together for a minilesson on revision, I told them that many writers revise by reseeing their writing—closing their eyes and picturing their stories and experiences in their minds' eyes—and then writing any new imagery they have pictured. After the minilesson, I sent the students back to their desks to try this strategy—to close their eyes and picture just the initial paragraph or two of their narratives. The teacher taped a blank piece of paper next to the first page of each original draft, and then asked the students to resee their writing and rewrite the beginnings of their stories without reading the originals.

As I walked around, I noticed that the difference in the two drafts was significant for many students.

In the original draft, Leo began his story like this (see Figure 6–4):

Figure 6–4 Leo's Draft

This is the Nick Hotel Water Park. They have a
100-gallon dunk tank and they have a huge
water slide and they have climbing nets.
Then when it was time to go, we trapped Jake
in the elevator.

After Leo closed his eyes, and pictured his story in his mind's eye, he revised the beginning of his narrative:

Figure 6–5 Leo's Revised Beginning

I climbed the silver bars and glided to the slide.
I slid down the slide. My spirit rose and I
bounced up when I hit the bottom.

The original draft of Leo's narrative is an outline of events, while the second draft *shows* rather than *tells* the events, helping the reader picture the story. He slowed the story down and, in his second draft, he also included how he, the writer, felt.

In the same class, Kyle revised his personal narrative using the same strategy (see Figures 6–6 and 6–7).

Figure 6–6 Kyle's First Draft

Draft 1

I was going home and got the Star Wars game after school. It was the first day it came out. I was so excited.

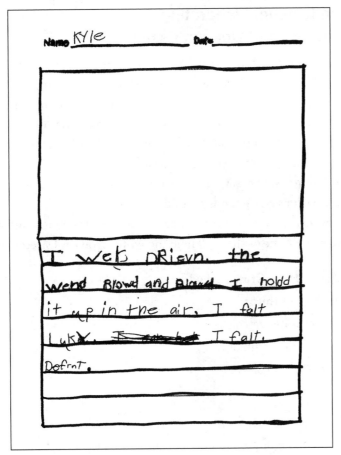

Figure 6–7 Kyle's Second Draft

Draft 2
*I was driving. The wind blew and blew. I held it
up in the air. I felt lucky. I felt different.*

In both examples, the writers transformed the beginnings of their writing by reseeing the experiences in their minds. Their revisions are large revisions—not just a changed word or two, but revisions in voice, emotion, and imagery. After revising the beginning of the piece, each of the writers went on to revise each subsequent paragraph of the original draft using the same strategy.

Revision Lesson: Elaborating in Persuasive and Opinion Essays

When students are writing essays, revision often consists of cracking open seed ideas. Most essay ideas start small and originate from an observation, an experience, or a thought. The real work of writing and revising an essay consists of growing that one small idea into something longer and more thoughtful, digging deeper, and elaborating and holding onto it for longer stretches of writing. Many young essayists' ideas are underdeveloped, and so the work of revising essays is to open up those ideas and, like peeling an onion, to discover layer upon layer of deeper thinking.

Start by giving each student a sheet to keep next to her as she writes an essay with some phrases that will help the writer grow and stretch her ideas.

Phrases to Help Grow Essay Ideas

An example of this is . . .

Another example of this is . . .

This makes me think of . . .

This reminds me of . . .

This shows . . .

Ask your students to write down an essay idea, an observation, or a thought on a piece of paper and write an equal sign next to it. Then, on a blank piece of paper taped next to the first piece, each student can crack open the idea or observation using some of the phrases that help writers grow ideas.

As students write their drafts, and grow their ideas, they can continue to use this strategy to keep adding more layers from their original thoughts or observations.

Revision Lesson: Elaborating in Informative or Explanatory Writing

Using precise details and words is essential in informative and explanatory writing as well as in other genres. Students can highlight vague words, phrases, and sentences and crack them open. You can give a minilesson that highlights detailed language in some favorite mentor texts (see the chapter on precise language in my 2013 book *Finding the Heart of Nonfiction: Teaching 7 Essential Craft Tools with Mentor Texts*) and make a comparison T-chart showing vague words, phrases, and sentences on the left side and the cracked-open, precise words on the right side, such as in Figure 6–8. Students can then highlight and clarify any vague words, phrases, and sentences in their own informative or explanatory writing.

FROGS

Vague Words	Precise Language
A toad eats insects.	A toad hops around after dark, snapping up moths, beetles, and crickets. It may eat more than 5,000 insects during a single summer. (Bishop 2008, 17)

Figure 6–8 T-Chart from a Section of *Frogs* by Nic Bishop

Seven Revision Tools for Adding Words and Text

There are seven revision tools students can use to add text to their writing:

1. **Caret signs:** For minor additions, a student can squeeze in a word or two by writing a caret sign (^) next to a word and writing a word or two above it.
2. **Sticky notes:** If a student wants to add a little more text—a phrase or a sentence or two—the student can write it on a sticky note and place the note on the page next to where the text should be added.
3. **Spider legs:** When a student wants to add several sentences, the student can write text on a "spider leg" (a long strip of paper) and tape it next to the place where it should be added.

4. **Blank pages:** For large amounts of text—paragraphs or a page—a student can tape a blank page next to the original page, draw an arrow from the text, and write new text on the blank page.

5. **Asterisks:** A student can also write an asterisk with a number or letter next to where the student wants to add text and then write new text on a blank page with the corresponding letter or number.

6. **Circles:** Students can use circles for revision in several different ways: They can circle words, phrases, or sentences that they need to come back to and revise at a later time. They can circle chunks of writing and place asterisks next to them when they need to move them to other parts of their texts. They can circle words, phrases, and lines that they're not sure about so they can return and reread them.

7. **Arrows:** A student can use arrows to show where to move one particular part of the writing, similar to the way a writer might use an asterisk. A student can also use an arrow if she runs out of space on a page to show that the writing continues on the back of a page or into the margins of the paper.

Verbs: The Engines of Sentences

The more specific the verb, the more energy and impact the sentence will have. Using a particular verb can go a long way in creating a scene or an image or in making a powerful argument. For example, instead of writing, "A bird *flies* in the sky," we could write, "A bird *soars* in the sky," or "A bird *flutters* in the sky." Each of these three different verbs—*flies*, *soars*, and *flutters*—gives the reader a different image: *flies* gives me a kind of generic image of a bird; *soars* gives the image of a hawk or other large bird slowly riding the wind; and *flutters* gives me a picture of a smaller bird, perhaps a starling or a swallow.

Similarly, "A horse *jumps*" can become instead "A horse *leaps*" or "A horse *vaults*." Although the images don't change much with these three verbs, the tone and sound of the words do.

When choosing specific verbs, writers select according to meaning, image, and sound. The right verb can eliminate the need for too many extra words as well.

Amy, a third grader, decided to reread the beginning of her narrative draft with the lens of words—particularly, the lens of verbs. Her objective was to focus on her verbs, although at a later time she used other lenses to revise her narrative:

> *Last weekend, I* ~~got to go~~ **drove** *to the park with my mom, dad and brother. We* ~~took~~ **brought** *a picnic lunch. When I got there, my brother* ~~went~~ **raced** *to the swings. The swings are his favorite. I played on the swings too while my mom and dad* ~~watched~~ **stared** *and smiled. They told us to be careful when we* ~~got~~ **soared** *too high.*

Although the revisions are simple, this writer showed an understanding and awareness of how revising weaker verbs can strengthen a piece of writing.

As a general rule of thumb for all genres, I ask students to revise making sure to avoid verbs that convey no sense of action: *have*; *do*; *make*; and forms of the verb *to be*.

Revision Lesson: Choosing Specific Verbs in Any Genre

Ask your students to make a list of all the possible verbs that could fit into the blank space in this sentence:

> The dog _____ across the yard.
>
> Examples: *runs, leaps, dashes, sprints, bounds, hurries, crawls, bolts, races, rushes, darts, charges*

Discuss how all of the above verbs are descriptive and concrete, yet each one gives the sentence a different connotation. For example, "The dog *leaps* across the yard" conveys a different meaning than "The dog *charges* across the yard." The change in verb is subtle and yet crucial. A dog that *charges* across the yard might suggest a dangerous dog, or at the very least perhaps a hungry dog charging toward its food, while a dog that *leaps* connotes a happy dog. Ask students to visualize and discuss the changes each verb makes to the meaning of the sentence.

Then ask them to highlight concrete and vivid verbs in their favorite texts to bring in to share with the whole class or their partners. One of my favorite passages that use wonderfully vivid verbs is a description of sports from Scott Russell Sanders' *Secrets of the Universe: Scenes from the Journey Home*:

> The game of catch, like other sports where body faces body, is a dialogue carried on with muscle and bone. One body speaks by *throwing* a ball or a punch, by *lunging* with a foil, *smashing* a backhand, *kicking* a shot toward the corner of the net; the other replies by *swinging, leaping, dodging, tackling, parrying, balancing.* (1992, 29; emphasis mine)

Or students can use the genre-specific examples that follow for an exercise in verb awareness.

Students can also select a piece of their writing and underline or highlight the verbs. Ask them each to brainstorm or look in a thesaurus, online or print, for alternative verbs and see if they can make the engines of their writing more powerful.

Although we don't want to turn writing into a prescriptive exercise and require students to use specific verbs for specific genres, I do think having a list of possible genre-specific verbs at their fingertips can be helpful in expanding their repertoires.

Following are several genre-specific tips about verbs.

Revision Lesson: Selecting Verbs for Narrative Writing

One of the exercises I give to students when they're writing narratives is to take a piece of paper and illustrate the action, and then write down as many verbs as they can that depict that action. For example, let's say I'm writing a piece about football and in my piece I describe how the quarterback throws the ball. I can draw a sketch of the quarterback throwing the ball and then beside it write a list of verbs that might show that action: *throw, hurl, toss, sling, propel, launch, lob,* and so on. As I work on my piece, I'll have a list of possible verbs to use. If students choose to use a thesaurus for this exercise, make sure that they reflect on the word connotations before they choose a word. The exercise is meant to grease the vocabulary wheel so that as students write, they realize that there are myriad possibilities for the verbs they choose.

Here is another exercise using a short poem that will help students reach for alternative verbs. I ask students to come up with at least two strong verbs to replace each of the neutral verbs written in bold in the first stanza of my poem "The Pencil Sharpener":

> The pencil sharpener
> **makes**
> the pencil
> into a sharp point
> and **leaves**
> the leftovers out.

Now here's the first stanza of my original poem. How do the stronger verbs change this poem?

> The pencil sharpener
> **chews**
> the pencil
> into a sharp point
> and **spits**
> the leftovers out.

Revision Lesson: Selecting Verbs for Persuasive and Opinion Essays

Verbs that analyze rather than summarize are most effective when writing a persuasive or an opinion essay. Writers also choose more formal words when writing essays, such as the verbs listed below:

suggests	hints (at)
asserts	implies
demonstrates	evokes
establishes	questions
explores	supports

For example, instead of writing,

> These research findings say . . .

a student might choose one of these alternatives:

> These research findings suggest . . .

> The frog scientist's research demonstrated . . .

When writing essays and using supporting evidence from quotations, students might use words from this list of possible verbs:

denotes	reveals
conveys	suggests
illustrates	determines
highlights	explains

For example, instead of writing,

> There *is* a side of John Adams that most readers didn't know.

a student might write,

> The author, David McCullough, *reveals* a side of John Adams that most readers didn't know.

Revision Lesson: Selecting Verbs for Informative or Explanatory Writing

When writers of informative and explanatory texts include evidence from research to support facts or points, they can revise verbs to give a more formal and authoritative tone. The following is a short list of verbs that work well to express the significance of evidence:

tells (us)   informs (us)

illustrates   indicates

confirms   suggests

proves

For example, instead of writing,

> This *is* a graph of climate change.

a student could write,

> The graph *confirms* climate change.

When writers of informative and explanatory texts include evidence from experts, and other people, to support their points, they might use speaking verbs that give a more formal tone, such as the ones on this list:

argues   believes

claims   explains

reports   demonstrates

states   acknowledges

shows (us)

For example, instead of writing,

> Scientists *say* that global warming has caused climate change.

a writer could choose from the list of verbs above:

> Scientists *acknowledge* that global warming has caused climate change.

Nouns: The Wheels of Sentences

If verbs are the engines of sentences, then nouns are the wheels on which the engines ride. Nouns need to be sturdy, solid, and specific. Using vague nouns like *stuff* and *thing* will flatten any sentence and force it to a halt. Using a general version of a noun instead of a more specific one can also slow a sentence down and cause the reader to lose interest. Revising with an eye toward making nouns more concrete and specific is essential. A concrete noun refers to objects that you can experience with your five senses.

Students should also know when and how to use abstract nouns. Abstract nouns identify concepts, feelings, experiences, and ideas. It would be very difficult to write a persuasive or literary essay using only concrete nouns. A combination of the two usually works well.

Revision Lesson: Choosing Specific Nouns

Sometimes it's easier to revise somebody else's words before we revise our own—it's less personal and easier to spot what needs to be revised.

As a whole class, or in partnerships, ask your students to replace these vague nouns with concrete nouns:

> **Example**
>
> The *thing* broke down. (original)
> The *air conditioner* broke down. (specific noun)
>
> She placed some *stuff* in her bag.
> I hear *something* out my window.
> She bought some *things* at the store.
> The *flower* smelled sweet.
> I saw a *bird* in the sky.

Then ask each student to select one of his or her own pieces of writing and replace the vague nouns with more specific and concrete ones.

Revising Word Choice: Denotation and Connotation

I love Mark Twain's quote that begins this chapter—"The difference between the almost-right word and the right word is the difference between the lightning bug and the lightning"—because it expresses so perfectly how finding the right word matters. When I write anything, whether it's an email, an article, or a book, I spend a lot of time rereading my words and attempting to fine-tune not just my words' denotation (the literal meaning of a word) but also their connotation (an association that a word evokes). Choosing the right word can not only convey a precise meaning but also give the reader a sense of the writer's voice, feeling, or opinion. Paying attention to connotation can add clarity, conciseness, and specificity to writing.

Revision Lesson: Paying Attention to Denotation and Connotation

Following are some sentences where a change in a verb or a noun changes the connotation of the sentence. Rereading and revising their writing by paying particular attention to the connotation of their words is a subtle yet critical skill for students to learn.

Here are three sentences whose verbs convey two different political and social biases. Ask students to read each sentence and discuss, in either a large group or partnerships, what the writers' biases might be.

> The garment workers *are asking* for a 10 percent pay increase.
>
> The garment workers *are demanding* a 10 percent pay increase.
>
> (The word *asking* seems reasonable while *demanding* suggests a hint of aggression and the writer's negative bias.)

> I saw a *crowd* at the soccer match.
>
> I saw a *mob* at the soccer match.
>
> (*Crowd* is neutral while *mob* suggests troublemakers.)

There are over 2,000 *vagrants* in the city.

There are over 2,000 *homeless* in the city.

(*Vagrants* suggests a negative value judgment while *homeless* is neutral and more compassionate.)

You can also give your students sets of three different words that denote the same meaning and ask them to categorize the connotations as negative, neutral, or positive:

fragrance, stench, smell

sound, tune, noise

beast, animal, pet

Ask your students which word they would choose if they were writing about flowers: *fragrance*, *stench*, or *smell*? Or if they were writing about trash, would they use the word *fragrance*, *stench*, or *smell*? All three words denote the same meaning but connote different meanings.

As students turn to their own pieces to revise, they can reread with an eye toward finding the most precise and clear words to express what they think and feel. Encourage them to use thesauri and dictionaries to guide them in choosing the exact words.

Sentence Variation and Fluency

Gary Provost has the most wonderful quote about sentence variation:

> This sentence has five words. Here are five more words. Five-word sentences are fine. But several together become monotonous. Listen to what is happening. The writing is getting boring. The sound of it drones. It's like a stuck record. The ear demands some variety. Now listen. I vary the sentence length, and I create music. Music. The writing sings. It has a pleasant rhythm, a lilt, a harmony. I use short sentences. And I use sentences of medium length. And sometimes, when I

am certain the reader is rested, I will engage him
with a sentence of considerable length, a sentence
that burns with energy and builds with all the
impetus of a crescendo, the roll of the drums, the
crash of the cymbals—sounds that say listen to
this, it is important. (1985, 60–61)

My teachers used to instruct me to keep away from short sentences
and, instead, use longer, more complex sentences. While this is sometimes
appropriate, you can see from Gary Provost's quote that a long sentence is
not necessarily better than a short one, and vice versa. It's the combination,
the variety of sentence lengths, that makes a piece of prose musical and
interesting to the reader. A paragraph is like a poem in that you hear the ebb
and flow of the words.

Roy Peter Clark wrote an article in the *New York Times* titled "The
Short Sentence as Gospel Truth." He said, "Express your most powerful
thought in the shortest sentence. . . . A long sequence of short sentences
slows the reader down, each period acting as a stop sign. That slow pace
can bring clarity, create suspense or magnify emotion, but can soon become
tedious. It turns out that the short sentence gains power from its proximity
to longer sentences."

Let's return to the last paragraph of Lincoln's inaugural speech and look
at the length of his sentences. The first few sentences of the last paragraph
are short; I've arranged them in a list here to illustrate their brevity:

I am loath to close.

We are not enemies, but friends.

We must not be enemies.

Three short sentences are then followed by a medium one and then a
long one:

Though passion may have strained, it must not break our bonds
of affection.

The mystic chords of memory, stretching from every battle-field
and patriot grave to every living heart and hearthstone all over

this broad land, will yet swell the chorus of the Union, when again touched, as surely they will be, by the better angels of our nature.

His short sentences intend to make listeners pay attention by slowing down the pace and letting us know that this is important. He then follows the short sentences with a medium-length sentence, and then a long one, which is like a drumroll to our ears toward the end of his speech.

In the following example, a fourth-grade student, Bailey, wrote an informational narrative about a frog (see Figure 6–9). Although she felt her content was good, she understood that using the same sentence length, and opening each sentence with the same pronoun, *She*, was boring to the reader. Bailey's revision consisted of creating more variety in her sentences.

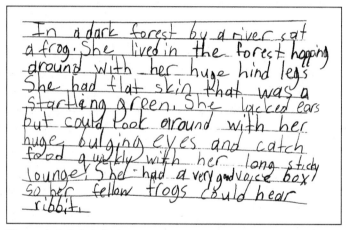

Figure 6–9 Bailey's Draft

Bailey's Revision

She lives in the forest hopping around with her huge hind legs. Easily seen because of her flat, startling green skin. Huge bulging eyes helped her look around and see better, and a long sticky tongue helped catch food quickly. If you hear the sound of ribbit, you know it's her—a frog with a very good voice box—that her fellow frogs can hear.

When Bailey revised, she changed sentence beginnings and combined sentences, which made for more sentence variety and less monotonous, choppy prose.

It's helpful for students to know that a few simple words can act as the glue that holds sentences together.

Sentence-Combining Words

- **Coordinating conjunctions:** *and, but, or, so, yet, nor*
- **Subordinating conjunctions:** *unless, because, even though, while, although, though, if, when, before*

Revision Lesson: Combining and Tightening Sentences

Sentence combining has to do with listening to the rhythm of your writing and altering the length of your sentences to keep them from being monotonous. Here are a few sentences that students can combine to make for more variety:

Example: *Combine the three short sentences below into one sentence.*

The wind blew hard. The ocean waves crashed. The rain came down in sheets.

The wind blew hard, the ocean waves crashed, *and* the rain came down in sheets.

Ask students to combine these sentences into one or two sentences using the conjunctions listed earlier.

Some dogs herd livestock. Some dogs are hunters. Some dogs guard homes. Some dogs perform police and rescue work.

In *Charlotte's Web*, Templeton is not a true friend to Wilbur. Templeton is not willing to help out when Wilbur's life is in danger.

The British colonists in America rebelled against Great Britain. Not every colony participated in the American Revolution.

Then ask students to return to their own writing and count the number of words in each sentence. This way they will see if their sentences are short or long or a combination of the two. Once they become aware of their sentence length, they can revise accordingly.

Partnership Revision Questions

One of the revision strategies I model for young writers is asking questions about a piece of writing as a way of discovering what's left out and what details and elaboration the writer might need to add. Although the example here is about elaboration, partnership work can be done with a variety of different foci, and teachers can choose how to direct a partnership's attention and questions.

Revision Lesson: Revising with Peers

The whole class can participate in this revision strategy, or it can be introduced in small partnerships. Ask a student author to choose a piece of writing that she would like to revise. Then ask her to read the writing aloud to the class, or to the group. Ask students in the audience, or in the rest of the group, to listen carefully and jot down any questions they might want to ask the author. Ask the author to leave the classroom for a few minutes. Ask your students to read the questions they wrote down aloud, and perhaps think of new questions they'd like to ask the author when she returns. Tell them to be sure they're open-ended questions that will get the writer to talk—not just yes-or-no questions. If you're doing this with the whole group, students can practice their questions with you, the teacher, in the role of the author. Then invite the author back into the room.

Students can then ask the author their questions with the goal of getting her talking about her piece of writing. Be sure to ask the author to bring a pencil or pen with her so if she decides that there is something she wants to add to her piece, she can mark it on her paper. The author might want to share with the class, or small group, what new information she'll add to her writing or any other revisions she'll make as a result of the audience's questions.

The CCSS include peer and partnership work in their grades 3–8 literacy standards as a means to revise. For example, here's a fifth-grade standard that mentions peer support:

> CCSS.ELA-Literacy.W.5.5. *With guidance and support from peers* and adults, *develop and strengthen writing as needed by* planning, *revising*, editing, *rewriting*, or trying a new approach. (emphasis mine)

A Yard Sale for Extra Words

I remember giving my first and last yard sale many summers ago. After weeks of procrastinating, my husband and I started to sift through old things to decide what to sell. This was no easy task. We are both collectors of junk, savers of newspapers and magazines, and we can think of excellent and valid reasons to save anything and everything we've ever owned. When I saw the things my husband was planning on throwing away, I asked him, "Are you sure you really want to throw that out?" to which he replied, "Well, you know, I was wondering if I should keep that." And he'd throw it into the save pile. He would ask me the same question, and by the end of our day we had collected more things in our save pile than in our giveaway pile.

Writers can't be pack rats with words. We can't save every word we've written. Maybe if we could have a yard sale with all those extra words, that would be an incentive to discard them. If I could put a one-dollar price tag on every extra *and* or *the* or *so* that I've cut out of my writing, I would be a wealthy person. But words, like all my old junk, need to be sorted out to see what we really need to keep and what needs to be thrown out.

Here's a general rule of thumb for students: be ruthless! Tell them to cut out all they can, but to save all their drafts in case they throw out too much and have nothing left because they've cut out everything. In *On Writing*

Well (2006), William Zinsser says that most pieces of writing can be cut down 50 percent without losing any of their true meaning or substance (16). Suggest that students delete pet words—these are words that we tend to use as a matter of habit.

E. B. White, in the introduction to *The Elements of Style*, wrote:

> The student learns to cut the deadwood from "this is a subject that," reducing it to "this subject," a saving of three words. He learns to trim "used for fuel purposes" down to "used for fuel." He learns that he is being a chatterbox when he says "the question as to whether" and that he should just say "whether"—a saving of four words out of a possible five. (Strunk and White 1979, xiv)

Revision Lesson: Getting Rid of Extra Words

Here's an example of an excerpt from a nonfiction book titled *Butternut Hollow Pond* in which I've added extra words:

Version with Unnecessary Words
As I take my morning walk I notice that the sunbeams fall in slender and thin shafts through a thick canopy of trees called swamp maples. The pond water is dappled in a confetti of pale and colorless sunlight. Wet dewdrops sparkle and shine on the reeds that grow in the water. (Heinz 2005)

Ask your students to practice cutting out extra words with this excerpt from *Butternut Hollow Pond*. Explain to them that they'll need to read the text carefully and cut out any unnecessary words. They might look to see what words are essential for this piece of writing.

Afterward, give them the original excerpt and discuss what words the author used and why.

Original Version

Sunbeams fall in slender shafts through the
canopy of swamp maples. The water is dappled in
a confetti of pale light. Dewdrops sparkle on the
reeds. (Heinz 2005)

The next step is for each student to choose a piece of his own writing
and cut out what he can. Then he can share his revisions with the rest of
the class.

Here are some suggestions for cutting out words and sentences:

- ▸ Don't overexplain.
- ▸ Don't tell us anything we already know.
- ▸ Don't put in details or information that might not be important to
  the scene or thesis you're writing.
- ▸ Cut out unnecessary words.

Word Strategic Conferences

The conferences in this section are typical conferences that occur when students are revising the words and sentences of their texts and will help you teach students how to revise effectively.

If You Find . . .

A student doesn't know what details to add:

> ‣ Read the draft out loud to the student, and suggest that he listen for places where he can "crack open" a word, phrase, or sentence. If the writer still can't find any places to add details, suggest one possible place that you might want him to crack open and tell him why. Then suggest he look for similar parts independently.
> ‣ Suggest the student close his eyes as you read a draft out loud to him to see if he can picture any new imagery and details that he could add.

A student doesn't know how to add details without copying over the entire draft:

> ‣ Show the student the seven revision tools for adding words and text (see pages 83–84) and let her choose one to use depending on how much text she wants to add.

A student has used general and vague words in a draft:

> ‣ Suggest that the writer try rereading the draft using the word lens. As he reads, he can highlight or underline any words that he wants to crack open.
> ‣ If the student is unsure what words are vague, select one word from the draft that he might want to strengthen, and model ways to do this—using a thesaurus and brainstorming alternative words in the margins of the paper, for example. Then suggest he find several more words that he could sharpen.

A student's sentences are all short and the same length:

▸ Explain how writers vary their sentence length to create more interest for the reader. Read the writing out loud to the student, emphasizing the shortness of each sentence, or suggest that she count the number of words in each sentence to see if they all contain a similar number of words. Ask if she can try combining her sentences to make longer ones.

Word Revision Checklist

- ❏ Have I checked over my words to make sure they are clear, precise, and concrete?

- ❏ Have I cracked open any words or sentences to find more vivid images, more concrete ways of describing?

- ❏ Are there parts in my writing that need more detail or elaboration?

- ❏ Are my verbs vivid and active?

- ❏ Are my nouns concrete?

- ❏ Have I reread my writing for sentence variation and fluency?

- ❏ Have I cut out unnecessary words?

CHAPTER 7

Revision Toolbox

Voice

It's my tone of voice. It's the writer's presence in the story.

—Jessica Anderson

My husband recently changed the greeting message on our answering machine. For years, whenever people called, they would hear the sweet, high voice of a young boy. One day my son said to us, "You really need to change that message on our answering machine because my voice doesn't sound like that anymore." He was right. His voice had changed so slowly over time, I wasn't even really aware that his voice was now a deep, fourteen-year-old's voice.

When we talk about voice in writing, I realize we're not talking about the actual sound of our voices—the pitch, the depth, and so on. But in the story about my son, both the sound of his voice had changed and also the words he used, his intonation—everything about his voice had changed to reflect the true teenager he was.

When I talk with students about voice, I describe it as the personality behind a writer's words. It's actually more than that—it's the heart, eyes, ears, tongue, and hands of the writer. It's a way of telling a story or poem. Voice can also include the voices of the different people we are inside and outside, the characters that speak to us in our heads, the purpose and audience for which we are writing, and the point of view we have chosen to write in.

Voice is difficult to teach because it's so subtle. Voice is what develops over time with students' gradual fluency in writing. If students aren't fluent writers, their voices cannot emerge. In my experience, poetry is a genre that can help students develop voice because poetry is emotional and personal, and students begin to develop their own unique ways of expressing their feelings and experiences when writing poetry. (See my 1999 book on teaching poetry, *Awakening the Heart: Exploring Poetry in Elementary and Middle School.*) Poetry also allows students a greater freedom than prose because it's short, it's manageable, and, most people think, it has no rules (it does, but they're different from the rules of prose). But students can also develop their voices by writing in other genres.

Genre, purpose, and audience also influence voice. If I'm writing an article for a newspaper, my voice will be different than it would be if I were writing a personal essay because my purpose and audience are different.

Here are several general suggestions when teaching voice:

- Students should write often—daily, if possible. The only way to develop voice is by becoming comfortable with writing and letting your words flow without being self-conscious.
- Students should write regularly about personal experiences and interests so that their words come from their hearts.
- Students shouldn't worry in the beginning about the skills of writing until they become more comfortable with letting their words flow.
- Encourage students to write letters to the newspaper or to politicians about issues that they're concerned about. Letter writing can help students come to know their own voices.
- Students should be aware of who their readers are and whether their pieces require an informal or a formal voice.

The revision strategies in this Revision Toolbox encompass a wide range of lessons about voice, from determining which point of view we should write in, to developing a more natural, authentic voice, to writing a character's voice, to adopting a more formal tone when our purpose and audience require us to.

Letting Purpose and Audience Drive Voice

If the queen of England asked me, "How are you today?" I would answer her in a formal way and say something like, "Very fine, Your Majesty, thank you. And you?" On the other hand, if I were sitting in Starbucks and a good friend walked up to me and asked me the same question—"How are you?"—it would sound very odd if I replied in the exact same way as I would to the queen. Instead, I would probably say something informal like, "I'm doing great! Just sitting here killing time—reading the Sunday *New York Times*—waiting for my son to finish his appointment. Do you want to join me?" We instinctively change our voices depending on our circumstances and situations. Similarly, our writing voices change depending on our purpose and audience. It's important to know what kinds of writing demand a more formal voice and what kinds call for a more informal voice and tone.

Speaking to Someone Who Is Really There

Often in narrative writing we want our voices to sound like ourselves speaking naturally. One strategy a student can use to help his natural voice emerge is to imagine that his best friend is in the room with him, and that the student wants to tell his friend a story of something he's experienced. How would the writer begin to tell his friend? What would his voice sound like? My guess is that his voice would have a lot of energy and excitement in it, and he would give just the right amount of details to build suspense and re-create the experience for his friend.

One of the revision strategies I use frequently is to speak my writing aloud as if my best friend were in the room with me. As I'm saying my words out loud, I ask myself these questions about my writing: Does my writing sound authentic? Does my writing sound like I could actually be speaking to someone who is really there?

Writing as though we are speaking to a friend gives our words solidity. We can borrow the energy of real speech to see how we can revise our own writing.

Revision Lesson: Speaking to Your Best Friend

Ask each of your students to choose a piece of writing that she would like to revise. At home, or in class, have each student speak her writing to her best friend or someone who is close to her. Ask the writer to speak part of the writing from memory, without reading the actual written text. If it's a long text, ask the student to speak the beginning from memory to try on this authentic voice. The student should have a pen handy to write down whatever insights this revision strategy reveals.

Using a Formal Voice

Some informational writing and essays require a more formal voice and tone, because the purpose and audience are academic and the readers are people with whom you are not familiar. But a formal tone does not mean writing that's mechanical and stiff, as if written by a machine. Nor does it mean writing that lacks any voice at all, like many encyclopedia entries. A formal tone of voice can sound like a human actually talking but not like someone having a casual chat.

Revision Lesson: Speaking to an Audience

Students can reread their informational writing and essays to revise their tone and words to sound more formal. On a chart, show them a few tips to keep in mind as they reread and revise writing to a more formal style:

- Stay away from using first-person pronouns, such as *I* and *me*.
- Contractions are often used in more casual and informal writing, so avoid the use of contractions, such as *can't*, *wouldn't*, and *weren't*.
- Avoid slang expressions and informal diction, such as *OK*, *yeah*, and *awesome*.
- Avoid words like *great* and *really*.

- Use domain-specific vocabulary from your research.
- Use transition words such as *in addition, furthermore, similarly, moreover, therefore,* and *another*.

Choosing the Right Point of View

Point of view and voice are closely related but are not the same. Point of view is the lens the writer gives to the reader through which to view the material, and voice is the identity of the writer.

During the revision process, a writer can change the point of view to hear how different voices and viewpoints will change the tone and overall voice of a particular piece of writing. It's important for students to become aware of the different types of point of view available to them when they write and what genres are usually in which point of view. It's also important for students to keep a consistent point of view throughout their pieces.

Here are four choices when considering point of view.

FIRST PERSON When an author writes in the first person, he uses words like *I, we, me, us, my,* and *mine*. The tone is personal, and the writer becomes a character in the piece. Narratives, personal and persuasive essays, opinion pieces, memoirs, autobiographies, book reviews, travel writing, and, depending on the purpose and audience, informational texts are written in the first person.

SECOND PERSON Writing in the second person uses the pronouns *you* and *yours* to address the reader directly. The second-person point of view is compelling because readers feel an immediate connection to the writer, as though she is speaking directly to them.

Depending on the purpose and audience, some informational texts, personal and persuasive essays, and opinions pieces can be written in the second person.

THIRD-PERSON OBJECTIVE The third-person objective uses the pronouns *he* and *she*. This point of view describes things as they are seen from the outside. This presents a more formal and academic tone.

Informational texts, biographies, essays, and articles can be written in the third-person objective.

THIRD-PERSON OMNISCIENT With the third-person omniscient point of view, the voice of the writer knows everything there is to know. The writer can enter the minds of his subjects when writing.

Narratives, journalism, and biographies can be written in the third-person omniscient.

Revision Lesson: Trying Out Different Points of View

Ask each of your students to choose a piece of writing he or she has already worked on and reread with the lens of point of view. What type of point of view did the writer use? Is it consistent throughout? The student might like to try a different point of view. Sometimes changing the point of view can help us see our writing in a new way even if we return to the original point of view in the final draft.

Trying Out Different Selves

The word *persona* originates from the Greek word meaning "mask." This goes back to the ancient days when the Greeks put on plays and each new character would wear a different mask. Writing through a mask is a strategy that writers use all the time. I find it liberating to not always speak from my perspective and to try on different voices and masks. It's also an effective way to try to understand the experiences and thoughts of another person, who perhaps lived in a different time, or to try to understand someone with whom you disagree. Students can try writing nonfiction, especially historical narrative, from the perspective of a character to see what insights this can bring.

Revision Lesson: Writing with a Mask

Have you ever wondered what the wind would say if it had a voice? Or a subway traveling through a dark tunnel? Or, perhaps, a soldier in the midst of a battle in the Civil War? Whom would the wind, the subway, or the soldier talk to? What would their voices sound like if they spoke? What would they tell us?

Ask each student to think of something in nature that he or she loves or thinks is fascinating or beautiful: wind, clouds, trees, birds, rain, leaves. (Sometimes it's easier to begin with something in the natural world.) Now, each student should try speaking from the point of view of the natural feature he or she chose. Each writer can ask: "What would I say? To whom would I speak? What would my voice sound like?"

Sari, a second grader, put on the mask of a leaf and wrote this short piece from the leaf's point of view:

> *I'm a leaf dancing in the wind. The wind stops. I*
> *stop. I start dancing again. Swish Swosh I go. I*
> *pick up a brown leaf and dance.*

A seventh-grade student wrote a photo-essay from the persona, and in the voice, of a young girl who worked in a textile mill in the early 1900s after looking at a Lewis Hine photograph of a girl in the factory:

> *My name is Sophie. I'm not really sure how old I*
> *am or who my parents are but I have two broth-*
> *ers who I care a lot about but don't see them*
> *very much because they work in the coal mines*
> *to get more money, which I can't do because I'm*
> *a girl. Which means I have to work here in a*
> *textile factory.*

Students will be amazed at some of the new insights that this strategy will give them into what they're writing about.

Inviting a Roomful of Company: Including Effective Dialogue

Writing dialogue that matters and is truthful is an art that takes a good ear and a lot of practice. Most beginning writers include too much or extraneous dialogue in their narratives and, therefore, the dialogue is boring, and the reader's mind begins to wander. Dialogue is a great way to convey information about the characters and the story within the story. In some ways, you can change the old adage *show, don't tell* to *show through telling* when thinking about dialogue. After writing a draft, a student can highlight the dialogue in his narrative and ask himself, "What information does the dialogue give to the story? What does the dialogue show the reader?"

Revision Lesson: Writing Dialogue

I read one story written by a fourth grader once that went something like this:

> *"Hi! How are you?" said Sara to her friend Jeff.*
> *"I'm fine. How's your summer going?" said*
> *Jeff.*
> *"Fine," said Sara.*
> *"How's your summer going? Have you done*
> *anything fun?" said Jeff.*
> *"I went to camp for two weeks," said Sara.*
> *"I went to the pool every day," said Jeff.*
> *"Bye. See you later," said Sara.*
> *"Bye," said Jeff.*

Nothing really happens here. The reader never gets to know the characters.

One way to revise dialogue is to create a scene through images and a sense of place. Everything that Sara and Jeff said in the previous dialogue could be summed up in a few words:

> Sara and Jeff bumped into each other on the
> corner and began to chat about their summers.

In this revision strategy, the writer cuts out dialogue from a story, summarizes it, and creates a scene instead. Here is another example of dialogue that could be easily condensed into a one- or two-sentence summation.

> "I bet I'm the fastest," said Karen as she ran
> around the pool.
> "No! I'm the fastest," said Jo, her best friend.

The lifeguard blew his whistle. "Please! No running around the pool," he warned.

Summation: Karen and Jo started to race around the pool; then the lifeguard blew his whistle to stop them.

There has to be a reason to use dialogue. Most of the time it's to build a scene or to show a character. Look at the characters created with this dialogue from *The Ghost-Eye Tree*:

"But Mama'll know," I said. "We spilt a lot of milk."
"That doesn't matter," my sister said. "I'll put some water in the bucket. She'll never know the difference." (Martin and Archambault 1988, 22)

You might ask your students what this dialogue reveals about the characters.

Or look at this example from *Granpa*, by John Burningham (1991). I ask my students, "What does this dialogue reveal about the following characters?"

"When we get to the beach can we stay there forever?"
"Yes, but we must go back for our tea at four o'clock."

Keep in mind what Tennessee Williams said about dialogue: "I do a lot of talking to myself when I write, trying out the sound of dialogue. Neighbors must think I always have a roomful of company."

Other Tips About Dialogue

▸ Robert Frost wanted to capture the way the New England farmers spoke, so many of his poems are written completely in dialogue that reveals not only the farmers' speech patterns but their character as well. Remind students that *how* their characters speak reveals a great deal about them.

▸ Many nonfiction pieces use quotations, which aren't dialogue per se but serve a similar purpose: to show information and to reveal and support writing through voice. Quotes can strengthen writing by adding validity to information and adding a human touch.

Revision Lesson: Practicing Your Voice

To give students more practice, ask them to revise the sample below using one of the voice revision strategies and then turn to their own writing to revise using the same revision strategy.

Voice Revision Strategies

- ▸ Speak to someone who is really there.
- ▸ Change the point of view.
- ▸ Try on different selves (try writing from a persona).
- ▸ Write text as dialogue.

Revision Sample Writing

The two boys watched the fisherman fish on the rocks. A big wave crashed and almost swept one fisherman into the sea. Another fisherman's line began to tug and almost swept him away too.

Voice Strategic Conferences

The conferences in this section are typical conferences that occur when students are revising the voice of their texts and will help you teach students how to revise effectively.

If You Find . . .
A student has written dialogue that is a conversation but doesn't show the reader any new information about the story or character:

▸ Ask the student to highlight the dialogue in the piece. Have the student, in the margins, try to summarize in one sentence what information each section of dialogue is giving the reader about the character or story. If the writer has a difficult time doing this, model a summary, or perhaps help her see that the dialogue doesn't give enough information and therefore she needs to revise.

A student has written an informational piece in an informal tone and you're unsure whether to require him to revise it to a more formal tone:

▸ It depends on the audience, purpose, and requirements of the class. If you require the student to write in a formal voice, he can easily reread and revise, deleting contractions, slang, and informal language. However, sometimes writing in a more informal tone adds style and creativity to a piece of writing even if its audience is academic.

A student has written a piece that has no voice and reads more like an encyclopedia entry:

▸ Ask the student to retell in her own words all, or part of, the piece to you or to a writing partner. You, or the writing partner, can then write down her words as she speaks (tell her to speak slowly) and read them back to her to reveal how she spoke the words in her own voice.

▸ Ask the student to rewrite her piece on a blank piece of paper without looking at the original draft. Then place the original draft and the new draft side by side and compare the two. Usually, the new draft will have voice because the student will have written the information in her own words. If there are any bits of information she left out from the old draft, she can add them in her own words.

Voice Revision Checklist

- ❏ What kind of voice does my writing require—informal or formal?

- ❏ What point of view is my piece written in? Is it consistent throughout?

- ❏ Have I tried revising using another point of view?

- ❏ Have a tried writing my piece using a different persona or mask? How has that strategy changed my writing?

- ❏ Does my dialogue contribute to my story or reveal something important about my character?

- ❏ Does my dialogue sound authentic?

- ❏ Have I used quotations to support my writing?

Epilogue

This line from William Stafford's poem "Practice" has stayed with me all these many years: "Maybe it is all rehearsal . . . maybe your stumbling saves you." This stumbling—which is what revision is like for me: stumbling to express myself—is what my writing, and my life, demand. It means that we don't have to be perfect. It means that our writing can be messy, we can make mistakes, we can be blind and not know exactly where we are going and what we're trying to say, and then we can resee our way into clarity.

If we can embrace, and help our students embrace, the fact that all writing is just stumbling and practicing—practicing to speak what's really in our hearts and on our minds—then revision will become an amazing process of trusting ourselves to someday write the words we need to write.

APPENDIX A

Writers' Quotes About Revision

I find first drafts difficult. Very difficult. Painful. Torture. I find after so many books that if I don't worry about how I'm going to fill up the middle and think scene by scene and let it happen that way, it will be all right. If I think in terms of a whole book at the beginning, I panic.

      —Judy Blume

I dive into a story the way I dive into the sea, prepared to splash about and make merry.

      —E. B. White

One mechanical aid to achieving a critical eye is to read out loud, and I do. Hearing what I have written gives me a fresh way of seeing what I have written.

      —Elaine Konigsburg

The main thing I try to do is write as clearly as I can. Because I have the greatest respect for the reader, and he's going to the trouble of reading what I've written—I'm a slow reader myself and I guess most people are—why, the least I can do is to make it as easy as possible for him to find out what I'm trying to say, trying to get at. I rewrite a good deal to make it clear.

      —E. B. White

Sculptors are always saying they see the statue within the block of granite or marble before they start. I love that metaphor, but I don't see it that way. [My goal] is to chip away the marble—the stack of manuscript pages—and reveal the statue.

      —Mel Gussow

I'm happy when the revisions are big. I'm not speaking of stylistic revisions, but of revisions in my own understanding.

—Saul Bellow

Maybe I revise because it gradually takes me into the heart of what the story is about. I keep trying to see if I can find that out.

—Raymond Carver

I went through three 500-sheet packages of the yellow paper and thirty or more soft black lead pencils. I used all 1,500 sheets but ended up with less than 500 pencil pages, so I guess I did constant rewriting as I went along.

—Helen MacInnes

By the time I am nearing the end of a story, the first part will have been reread and altered and corrected at least one hundred and fifty times. I am suspicious of both facility and speed. Good writing is essentially rewriting. I am positive of this.

—Roald Dahl

Interviewer: How much rewriting do you do?

Hemingway: It depends. I rewrote the ending of *Farewell to Arms*, the last page of it, thirty-nine times before I was satisfied.

Interviewer: Was there some technical problem there? What was it that had stumped you?

Hemingway: Getting the words right.

—Ernest Hemingway,
"Ernest Hemingway, the Art of Fiction No. 21"

Now I see *revision* as a beautiful word of hope. It's a new vision of something. It means you don't have to be perfect the first time. What a relief!

—Naomi Shihab Nye

APPENDIX B

Revision Survey

Name: _____

What is revision?

_____

_____

_____

_____

_____

_____

How do you feel about revising? Do you like to revise your writing? Why or why not?

_____

_____

_____

_____

_____

_____

Please describe one example of a revision technique that you've used in the past.

_____

_____

_____

_____

_____

_____

APPENDIX C

Peer Conferring Revision Questions

Ask the writer:

1. What was it like for you to write this piece? Did you have any problems while writing?

2. What do you think you need to work on in your writing?

3. How can I help you? Are there any parts you want me to pay close attention to as I read or listen to your writing?

4. Are there any places where you can add more?

5. What is the focus or heart of your piece?

6. What will you work on next?

APPENDIX D

Webbing Template

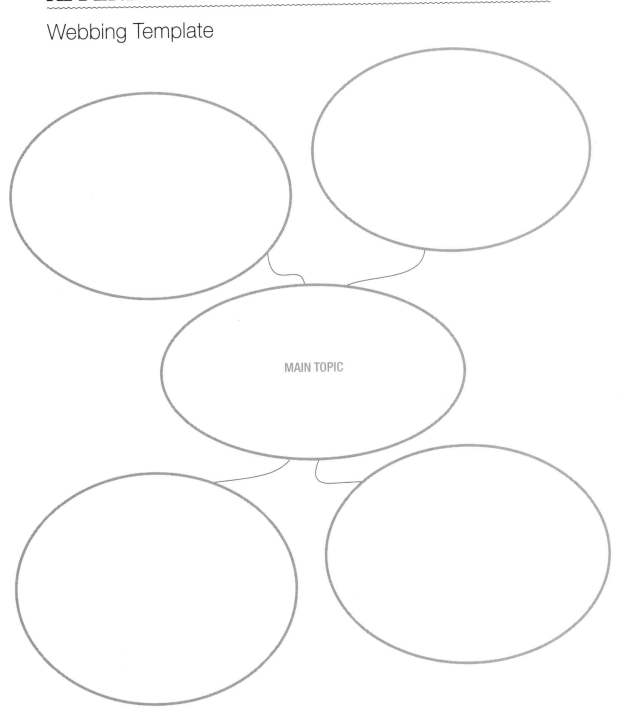

MAIN TOPIC

APPENDIX E

Story Mountain Template

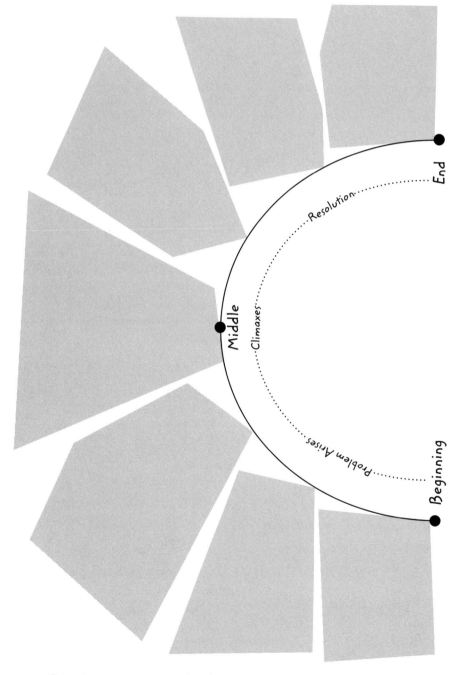

APPENDIX F

Essay Template

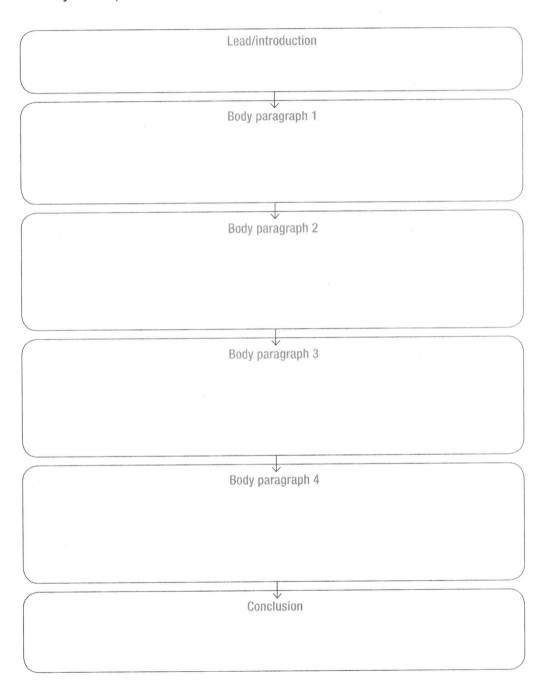

Lead/introduction

Body paragraph 1

Body paragraph 2

Body paragraph 3

Body paragraph 4

Conclusion

APPENDIX G

Sequence Template

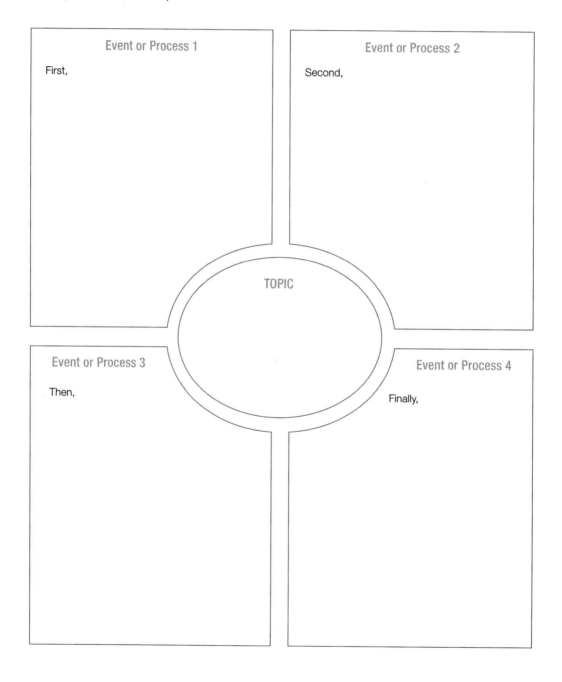

APPENDIX H

Compare-and-Contrast Template

```
┌─────────────────────────────────────────────────┐
│                                                   │
│                                                   │
│                                                   │
│                                                   │
└──────────────┬────────────────────┬──────────────┘
               │                    │
┌──────────────┴───────┐  ┌────────┴──────────────┐
│        Alike         │  │      Different         │
│                      │  │                        │
│                      │  │                        │
│                      │  │                        │
│                      │  │                        │
│                      │  │                        │
│                      │  │                        │
│                      │  │                        │
│                      │  │                        │
│                      │  │                        │
└──────────────────────┘  └───────────────────────┘
```

APPENDIX I

Cause-and-Effect Template

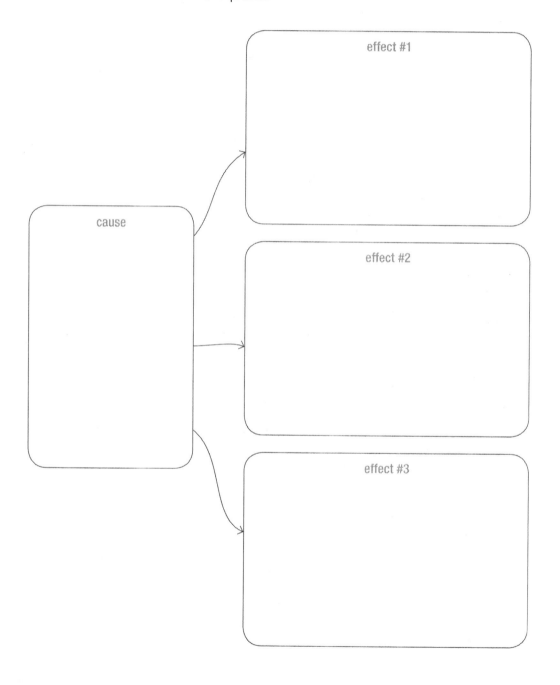

APPENDIX J

Problem-and-Solution Template

Problem

Solution

APPENDIX K

Description Template

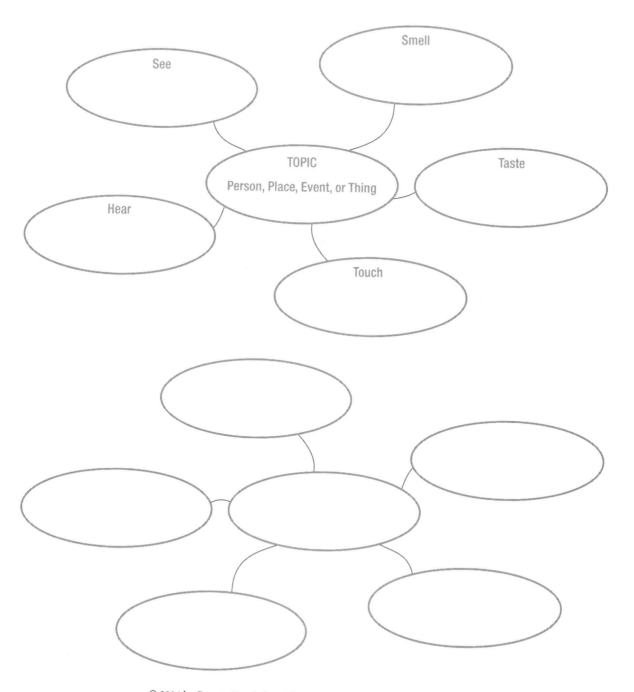

APPENDIX L

Revisions of My Poem "Dragonfly"

Here's a poem that was published in one of my children's books, *Creatures of Earth, Sea, and Sky*, which I originally wrote in my writer's notebook. (Even if your students aren't writing poetry, they can read the revisions I made here, and try to name the revision strategies. Then, with similar strategies they can try revising their writing—in any genre. If they are writing poems they can try revising their poems first before they tackle longer texts. Poetry is short and more manageable and, therefore, easier to revise.)

Dragonfly (First Draft)

Your wings stretch out like a paper kite.

You skim the pond's surface feeding

on gnats, mosquitoes and flies.

You are deep violet,

and a bright blue.

You can see so much with your 25,000

angles to your eyes.

You're like a helicopter

with two pairs of wings that

move in different directions.

Your wings are mostly clear

with splotches of color

like miniature stained glass windows.

In the first draft of "Dragonfly," I was trying to integrate some of the factual information from my research about dragonflies into the poem (for example, the dragonfly has 25,000 angles to a single eye) and to describe what I noticed about the dragonfly as I remembered it landing on the dock next to me. I wanted to write the first draft of "Dragonfly" in the second person, as a "letter" poem, to make the poem more intimate, but I ended up changing that in my final draft.

I try not to judge my first drafts too harshly—or declare they're finished to soon. My first drafts are valuable to me as I reread them for rich lines, good metaphors, or places to expand.

I liked the helicopter and stained-glass-window similes because they felt true—a dragonfly really does look like a helicopter, and its wings do look like stained glass. I decided to change the point of view to see what this would do for the voice of the poem. As much as I liked the factual information that dragonflies have 25,000 angles in one eye, I needed to cut that out because it didn't fit here.

Dragonfly (Second Draft)

She skims the pond's surface like a

helicopter searching for gnats,

mosquitoes and flies.

The best flier in the insect world.

Her reed body is colored with blue.

I stopped writing in the middle of my second draft because I didn't like the way the draft was going. "The best flier in the insect world." I don't think so! For me, revising sometimes means starting each draft over again from the beginning without being too critical of myself.

Dragonfly (Third Draft)

She skims the pond's surface skin

searching for gnats, mosquitoes and flies.

Her wings outspread

blur with speed.

As her reed like body lifts off the ground like a small plane,

she then touches down

to pick up her prey.

She stops to sun herself on the dock

her wings still.

They look like stained glass windows

with the sun shining through.

The poem was almost there. I had the ending with the stained-glass-window metaphor. And I liked the helicopter, now turned to a plane, metaphor but thought perhaps I didn't need to say it explicitly but just imply it with fewer words, such as "blur with speed" and "touches down." I also needed to do some pruning and neutralize the point of view.

Here's the final draft:

Dragonfly

It skims the pond's surface,

searching for gnats, mosquitoes, and flies.

Outspread wings blur with speed.

It touches down

and stops to sun itself on the dock.

Wings flicker and still:

stained-glass windows

with sun shining through.

When I review all of my drafts of "Dragonfly," I can list the revision strategies I used to write this one small poem.

Can your students find each revision strategy that I name on this list in the drafts of "Dragonfly"?

- ▸ Write multiple drafts.
- ▸ Change the point of view.
- ▸ Select strong words.
- ▸ Delete extraneous details.
- ▸ Select vivid images.
- ▸ Delete extra words.
- ▸ Rearrange words.
- ▸ Change line breaks.

APPENDIX M

Seward's Draft and Lincoln's Revision

Seward's Draft

I close. We are not, we must not be, aliens or enemies, but fellow-countrymen and brethren. Although passion has strained our bonds of affection too hardly, they must not, I am sure they will not, be broken. The mystic chords which, proceeding from so many battle-fields and so many patriot graves, pass through all the hearts and all the hearths in this broad continent of ours, will yet again harmonize in their ancient music when breathed upon by the guardian angels of the nation.

—William Henry Seward, quoted in *Team of Rivals: The Political Genius of Abraham Lincoln*, by Doris Kearns Goodwin

Lincoln's Revision

I am loath to close. We are not enemies, but friends. We must not be enemies. Though passion may have strained, it must not break our bonds of affection. The mystic chords of memory, stretching from every battle-field and patriot grave to every living heart and hearthstone all over this broad land, will yet swell the chorus of the Union, when again touched, as surely they will be, by the better angels of our nature.

—Abraham Lincoln, quoted in *Team of Rivals: The Political Genius of Abraham Lincoln*, by Doris Kearns Goodwin

Works Cited

Bishop, Nic. 2008. *Frogs*. New York: Scholastic.

Burningham, John. 1991. *Granpa*. New York: Dragonfly Books.

Carver, Raymond. 1989. *Fires: Essays, Poems, Stories*. New York: Vintage.

Coelho, Paulo. 2006. *The Alchemist*. New York: HarperCollins.

Davies, Nicola. 2001. *Bat Loves the Night*. Cambridge, MA: Candlewick.

————. 2003. *Surprising Sharks*. Cambridge, MA: Candlewick.

Fitzgerald, F. Scott. 2007. *The Great Gatsby*. Read by Anthony Heald. Ashland, OR: Black-stone Audio. Audiobook, 4 compact discs; 5 hrs.

Fletcher, Ralph. 2011. *Mentor Author, Mentor Texts: Short Texts, Craft Notes, and Practical Classroom Uses*. Portsmouth, NH: Heinemann.

Follet, Ken. 2002. "Interview: December 6, 2002." By Bookreporter. Available at www.bookreporter.com/authors/ken-follett/news/interview-120602.

Gershwin, Lisa-ann. 2013. *Stung! On Jellyfish Blooms and the Future of the Ocean*. Chicago: University of Chicago Press.

Goodwin, Doris Kearns. 2006. *Team of Rivals: The Political Genius of Abraham Lincoln*. New York: Simon and Schuster.

Hairston, Maxine, John Ruszkiewicz, and Christy Friend. 2002. *The Scott, Foresman Handbook for Writers*, 6th ed. New York: Longman.

Heard, Georgia. 1999. *Awakening the Heart: Exploring Poetry in Elementary and Middle School*. Portsmouth, NH: Heinemann.

————. 2013. *Finding the Heart of Nonfiction: Teaching 7 Essential Craft Tools with Mentor Texts*. Portsmouth, NH: Heinemann.

Heinz, Brian J. 2005. *Butternut Hollow Pond*. Minneapolis: First Avenue Editions.

Hemingway, Ernest. 1958. "Ernest Hemingway, the Art of Fiction No. 21." Interview by George Plimpton. *Paris Review* 18 (Spring). Available at www.theparisreview.org/interviews/4825/the-art-of-fiction-no-21-ernest-hemingway.

Kaplan, Robert. 1999. *The Nothing That Is: A Natural History of Zero*. New York: Oxford University Press.

MacLachlan, Patricia. 1980. *Through Grandpa's Eyes*. New York: Harper and Row.

Martin, Bill Jr., and John Archambault. 1988. *The Ghost-Eye Tree*. New York: Square Fish/Henry Holt.

McPhee, John. 2012. "John McPhee, the Art of Nonfiction No. 3." Interview by Peter Hessler. *Paris Review* 192 (Spring). Available at www.theparisreview.org/interviews/5997/the-art-of-nonfiction-no-3-john-mcphee.

National Governors Association (NGA) Center for Best Practices and Council of Chief State School Officers (CCSSO). 2010. *Common Core State Standards for English Language Arts and Literacy in History/Social Studies, Science, and Technical Subjects*. Washington, DC: NGA Center for Best Practices and CCSSO.

Provost, Gary. 1985. *100 Ways to Improve Your Writing*. New York: Signet.

Sanders, Scott Russell. 1992. *Secrets of the Universe: Scenes from the Journey Home*. Boston, MA: Beacon Press.

Strunk, William Jr., and E. B. White. 1979. *The Elements of Style*. 3d ed. New York: Macmillan.

Temple, Emily. 2013. "20 Great Writers on the Art of Revision." Flavorwire.com, 8 Jan. Available at http://flavorwire.com/361311/20-great-writers-on-the-art-of-revision/.

Wagner, Tony. 2012. *Creating Innovators: The Making of Young People Who Will Change the World*. New York: Scribner.

Wilson, Reid. 2013. "How Three Weeks in New Zealand Changed My Relationship with Food: A Journey from Table to Farm." *Atlantic* (October): 43. Available at www.theatlantic.com/magazine/archive/2013/10/from-table-to-farm/309449/.

Winter, Jeanette. 2011. *The Watcher: Jane Goodall's Life with the Chimps*. New York: Random House Children's Books.

Zinsser, William. 2006. *On Writing Well: The Classic Guide to Writing Nonfiction*. New York: HarperPerennial.

Index